The Social Resource

Translating Social Media into Business

D1732105

Sharad Gandhi

Christian Ehl

Dedication

I dedicate this book to my family:
My parents, who have enabled me, my wife Lisa,
who is encouraging me, our son's Philip and Vincent,
who have taught me everything I know about social.
Thanks also to my team at Hillert und Co.
You are my social resource!

- Christian Ehl

I dedicate this book to my children:
Samay – for spiritual insights and strength from within me;
Mona Lisa – for courage to pursue, in spite of all odds.

- Sharad Gandhi

Contents

Acknowledgments

We want to thank our Social Resource who helped in making this book possible. Valerie Kathawala for professional editing. Claudia Schmidt and Nico Rausch for the graphics. Priyanka Boghani, Marta DeBellis, Oliver Gajek, Peter Greischel, Bernhard Oberlechner, Doris Eichmeier, Raza Zaidi and John-Paul Herrmann for critically reviewing the manuscript and for providing very useful suggestions for improvements. Our special thanks go to all employees of Hillert und Co. Interactive und Mobile Marketing GmbH for their encouragement and support.

- Christian Ehl
- Sharad Gandhi

Introduction

Imagine having the capability to engage the best minds in the world, working together in your interest, driven by their own motivation, helping you to accomplish your business success. This book shows you how to achieve this.

We have made a very interesting discovery. All of us – people and businesses – possess a secret resource: the social resource. It is a resource, like other familiar resources – capital, real estate, raw materials, employees, experts and knowledge – that we must first realize we possess, and then learn how to use. Your social resource is the network of people you know and who share your vision, which you can align with your mission and activate to attain your goals.

We believe that the power of the social resource provides businesses with enormous transformational efficiencies in almost all areas, including manufacturing, product innovation, hiring, employee development, customer service, marketing, sales and business intelligence.

Internet-based social media tools and platforms such as Facebook, Google+, LinkedIn and Twitter provide unique opportunities to harness this social resource to achieve your business goals efficiently. Essentially, the social resource captures the power of your social network's members – their knowledge, insights, skills, capabilities, and networks – and puts it to use for the benefit of your mission.

The power of the social resource allows you to achieve amazing results, through social networking and social media. This holds both for businesses and individuals in running a business. Our goal in writing this book is to share with you the tremendous power of your social resource: what it is, how it works, how to develop it and how to use for achieving your business goals.

Today, social media is mostly associated with consumers and personal communications. However, the mass communication mechanisms created by new social media platforms have already had a huge impact on the business, political and economic worlds. Many decision makers in corporations already feel that a major transformation in social communication is under way, one that will profoundly affect their businesses. However, many do not know how to leverage the new social networks to their advantage for their businesses.

This book is intended to address the needs of businesses, especially business decision makers, helping them to realize the potential of their social resource and how to capitalize on it. In social networks, the roles of the actual business and of individuals working for the business are tightly linked. Business individuals play a key role in making business networks function by interacting with other business individuals (employees, customers, partners, consultants, etc.).

People do business with people, as the saying goes. In this book, we often describe the actions and roles of business individuals acting on behalf of a business. For ease of understanding, we also show examples of how individuals use their social resources in their private or consumer lives. However, our intention is always to show how the business benefits from using its social resource.

Some clarification of terms is essential for understanding this book. The words "media" and "content" are often used interchangeably. Strictly speaking, media is a channel that provides content for its audience. Often, media is also used to include the content provided by the channel.

The terms "social media" and "social networking" are also often used interchangeably and this creates confusion. There is no unique definition of these terms, hence we will use a simple definition in this book: people interact with each other in social networks. The resulting collection of conversations, dialogs and content generated within the network by all the interactions is called social media. Moreover, social media will also be used to describe the entire category of Internet-based social interactions and content creation.

Here is a quick outline of the book: Chapter 1 explains in an illustrative fashion the origins of social media and the fundamentals of its workings in the business context. Chapter 2 shows what, exactly, the social resource is and how it can help you. Chapter 3 offers an overview of different lines of business in a company, such as manufacturing, service, marketing, sales, product development, etc. that may benefit from your company's social resource. Chapter 4 details the key elements for developing the social resource of your company. Chapter 5 illustrates with business examples how to put the social resource into action in a few different areas for your company. Chapter 6 concludes with an outlook on where social media may lead us in the future. The book offers many illustrations and examples to facilitate understanding.

We are both social media consultants, with engineering and marketing backgrounds. What brings us together is our fascination with and passion for the way technology is rapidly transforming our lives and businesses. We immensely enjoy sharing with others our insights into how individuals, society and businesses adopt and use new technologies. We have extensive experience in the multinational corporate world and in the innovation-driven start-up space.

We often see clients start projects in a hurry, without a clear understanding of goals and methods. They get engrossed in just getting things done. When we advise our clients, we believe it is very important for us to ensure that they start their projects with a "why?" before they debate "what?" to do in social media.

When business leaders have a clear vision of why they are doing what they are doing, it creates a powerful high-level sense of conviction, a commitment to a mission their customers can relate to emotionally and become a part of. Only after sorting out the "why?" do we lead the clients to the "how?" to achieve their mission. That formulates their strategy. Only then do we develop with the client "what?" exactly they can do to implement their defined strategy.

In fact, we call our consulting methodology "WOW!": Why? – How? – What? Over the years, we have observed that projects that start with a clear analysis and understanding of Why?, then sequentially develop How? and finally the What? of a project have a much better success rate.

For social media projects, we help clients first to explore their vision and understand why it will benefit them to engage in social media. Once we have jointly verbalized the Why?, we identify a social media program for a specific, critical area of our customer's mission. At that point, we jointly develop an overall strategy for how to realize that social media program. Only when the strategy, concept, design and plan are ready and approved do we start on What?, exactly, must be done to implement the social media program.

What is the "WOW!" for writing our book?

Why? – Our conviction that the Internet and social media are fundamentally transforming the social power balance in the world in the way we, as individuals and as a society, communicate our opinions. We use new platforms, tools, and devices and the technology of Internet-based social networks. We are fascinated by these changes and their impact on our daily lives and on the business world. Our passion for communicating our insights also strongly motivated us to publish them.

How? – We aim to communicate the "magic of social media transformation" in clear and simple language, to convey our own fascination, personal experience and insights to you, the business audience.

What? – We hope the book relays the fundamentals and origins of social media, its mechanisms, its business value and its uniqueness, as well as how to set it up and get the best out of it. Examples and illustrations are used to facilitate communication of the key concepts.

We have developed an understanding of social media and how it applies to businesses. This is the result of countless discussions, customer meetings, and workshops, as well as extensive reading. We have now compiled our experiences and insights into this book. We hope that it motivates you to apply it to your business and allows you to reap the tremendous potential of your social resource.

Christian Ehl & Sharad Gandhi

Here is where we started the book, in the village of Niederthai, 1800 meters up in the Austrian Alps.

1. Social Media – Origin, Evolution and Fundamentals

This chapter traces the origins and evolution of social media. Dynamics of social media processes are clarified to facilitate a basic understanding and lay the foundation for the main theme of this book: the social resource and how to use it.

The 2010 movie "The Social Network" and the 2011 political revolution in Egypt have made "social media" and "social network" household terms. With 800 million out of more than 2 billion Internet users owning a Facebook account as of September 2011, the growing assumption is that everyone knows social media and uses social networks in one form or another. The surprise is the pace at which social networking has grown, from very few users to hundreds of millions in the eight years since its inception.

In its physical form, social networking is nothing new. Neither is social media. Both have existed throughout history. Our urge to communicate is at the heart of human existence. Communication has always been a core human need. Historically, our survival has depended on our ability to communicate information about threats, food and shelter effectively and reliably. Humans are therefore willing to invest a lot to communicate well. We form face-to-face, physical social networks through which to exchange information and improve the dependability of the information each individual possesses. The information contained in these practical exchanges between people is social media – media generated by social communities.

Thousands of years ago there was of course no conventional published media as we know it today. All media was social media, generated by social interactions among members of communities. When communities intermingled, social media spread and was enhanced. This phenomenon of social media communication can be observed when groups of people meet, at gatherings or conferences such as the one shown in Figure 1.1. These are informal exchanges of information, views, opinions and experiences that we all listen to and learn from. Social media and social networking is very familiar. It is a trusted source of information that comes naturally to us. Social media is simply communication.

Figure 1.1: Classic social networking and social media

Social media and networking is very familiar, trusted and comes naturally to us. Social media is all about communication. It can be commonly observed whenever groups of people meet. These are informal exchanges of information, views, opinions and experiences that we enjoy and learn from.

Throughout history humans have refined how we communicate and deal with information. However, over the last 50 years, technology has radically improved our ability to exchange information.

There are four major dimensions to communication:

1. Media: which media do we consume?
2. Interaction: which means of interaction do we use to communicate?
3. Devices: which tools or devices do we use to communicate?
4. Infrastructure: what infrastructure is needed to support communication?

Let us look at each one of these to understand its role in communication.

The media imparted and consumed by humans when they lived in caves was limited to verbal exchanges among or between clans and, maybe, paintings in some caves. Conversations and storytelling were the primary modes of communication for thousands of years. The invention of written language marked the first revolutionary shift in media. It allowed the recording and storage of information and knowledge on stone, papyrus and paper. The tools used ranged from stones and chisels to charcoal and pencils. Religious institutions primarily provided the needed infrastructure in the form of temples, churches and sacred texts.

Media then remained fairly unchanged until the invention of the printing press by Guttenberg in the 16th century. This led to the first mass media. The printing press made it possible to create multiple copies of information for mass distribution and the printing press gave birth to publishing. However, the creation of media and publishing remained fairly restricted, resting in the hands of a few, for many years. The swiftest transformation of communication started with the advent of personal computers. Figure 1.2 illustrates the radical transformation and evolution of communication over the last 30 years, from a pre-PC era to today.

Information behavior influences	"1990" (1985-1995) →		"2000" (1995-2005) →		"2010" (2005-2015)
Media (Which public/published information is consumed)	TV, Magazines, CD-ROM, ...	+	Web www.xyz.com	+	Web 2.0 (User generated content)
Interaction (How interactions with others are conducted)	.doc, Letters, ...	+	name@email	+	Social Networks (Self organized communities)
Devices (User information interaction)	Desktop PC	+	Laptop, Mobile phones	+	Mobile Internet Devices (Always info-connected)
Infrastructure (Backbone for media and communication)	Local Servers	+	Internet, Servers	+	Cloud Computing (Data/apps always accessible)
Communication profile	Computerized →		Internet →		Socially Networked

Figure 1.2: Radical transformation of our communication profile

Communication of information is a fundamental human need born out of our survival instinct. The technology behind media, interactions, devices and infrastructure has evolved through history. The biggest technological changes have happened in the last few decades. As a result, the mainstream communication profile of society has developed from being computerized to being Internet centric to being socially networked. Interestingly, each time we take on a newer communication profile, we carry forward the previous communication habits for a few more decades, maybe out of inertia.

Figure 1.2 illustrates how the evolution of media type and the methods of interaction through modern communication devices have shifted the infrastructure of our communication profile from being computerized to being Internet oriented to being socially networked today. It is important to note that newer elements of communication are additive, complementing but not eclipsing the old. Although we read a lot on websites or via social media nowadays, we have not given up reading print media. We write emails, but we also send letters or cards – at least on special occasions. Let us look at the last two waves in a bit more detail.

The Internet wave (1995-2005) allowed every person, business and institution to create a global presence with a website. This was a tremendous change and liberated us from dependency on publishers. At the same time, the widespread adoption of email also allowed everyone to communicate freely with everyone else around the world. Laptops and mobile phones freed global communication from even more limits, giving people accessibility from anywhere, at anytime. The infrastructure consisted of software running on millions of Internet and communication servers, networked globally, without which, no communication would have been possible. People, businesses, institutions, and governments that communicated in this way were proud of the Internet adjective associated with their names.

The Internet age led developments in all four of these areas of media, interaction, devices and infrastructure and ushered in the next wave: the "social network" or "social media" wave (2005-2015). The tools and platforms necessary to generate media and publish became so easy to use and inexpensive that almost anyone could create and publish without professional help. Digital cameras and mobile phones allowed pictures and videos to be captured and posted on the Internet easily, adding another dimension to standard text. This phenomenon was given the name Web 2.0 and was mostly characterized by user-generated, multimedia content published on sites such as Flickr, Picasa and YouTube. Essentially, anyone could become a media creator and publisher.

Social networks, such as Facebook, allow anyone to become part of a self-selected community of friends. Through these, they can share their own media and comment on their friends' published media. This opportunity has created one of the most powerful features of social media: a rich dialog among community members. Social network platforms like Facebook and Google+ have become very popular for communication among groups because they allow social interaction in a variety of ways. Every time we post a link or update our status in such a forum, we are building a layer of social opinion on virtually any topic – a city, a restaurant, a movie, a book. Smart mobile devices like iPhones, iPads, and various Android and

Windows devices allow anyone to be on the network, consuming and publishing any time, anywhere. In the background, cloud computing fulfills the unique function of tying all of this information together in a transparent, auto-synchronizing fashion to make it work without the consumer having to understand or manage the computing and networking infrastructure. Cloud infrastructure gives the consumer multiple devices, all functioning in sync through the common information and computing base in the cloud. More and more of the computing infrastructure is moving in this direction.

Social media and social networking are creating a society in which people are constantly communicating and forming and sharing opinions through electronic media. This, in turn, is shaping how businesses, communities and governments operate and pursue success. Internet-based social media and social networking tap into the very same principle instincts of communication humans have always had, but make the experience global, instantaneous, inclusive and transparent. Social media is very powerful because it dramatically changes the power equations in society, placing power in the hands of the people who generate, publish and share their views openly and develop opinions that may be more genuine and representative of the society in which they live. Socially cultivated opinions have the power to bring down governments and companies, as recently evidenced in the case of Egypt and the BP oil spill. However, when used effectively, the social resource can be harnessed by companies and governments to make them highly competitive and successful. It provides them with a channel for direct dialog with their audiences and customers.

1.1. Social media business insights

Social media, which is generated by the social network, has a very powerful impact on our decision making, since it comes from a community of chosen friends or peers whom we trust (as compared to messages from vendors, who have a vested interest in trying to influence us). Companies are actually better off treating the social network as a customer and winning its approval. The social network can help win customers within the network by generating peer recommendations. The social network then becomes a new channel to your customers. It can amplify your messages, present them to your customers and win them for your business. It also "listens" to the genuine viewpoints of customers and gives you an integrated view of their honest perceptions and opinions. Finally, the social network and social media are unique in being a true opinion-building platform that allows an opinion to be developed on any topic via open discussions across the community. It creates total transparency by ruthlessly exposing the truth. The observations above can be summarized in four basic principles that characterize social media, especially for business:

1. Social network is the customer
2. Social channel is the consultative channel
3. Social network conversations allow listen-understand-dialog logic-talk
4. Social media is an opinion-building platform

1.1.1. Social network is the customer

Figure 1.3: Social network – your new customer to win
Every company tries its best to win customers by directly reaching out to them with their messages. However, customers are surrounded by their socially networked "friends," who have a much bigger influence on them. This means the best way to win customers is also to win their social networks and these will help win the customers.

Every business communicates with its customers to influence them and win them for its products, services and brand name. Influencing and understanding customers is a major goal of marketing and sales departments. Many innovative methods are put to use for influencing the customer's thinking and decision- making process through various channels: advertising points of sale, press, trade shows, etc. Most of the marketing effort is focused on directly messaging the customers.

Social networking and social media provide a new and more effective method of influencing customers: via their own social media "friends" (peers, community, family) on the social network. As we all know from experience, when our friends recommend a book, a movie or a restaurant, we are far more likely to go with their recommendations than a suggestion from an advertisement or a magazine. Statistically, our friends' influence on us is three to four times greater than that of vendors' messages. As a result, a vendor loses the battle for customer influence to the customer's social network.

This changes if the vendor focuses on winning the social network to win the customer. We believe that treating the customer's social network as a customer and winning it is the best approach for a vendor, shown in figure 1.3. The social network can become your ally and reinforce your messages to the customer. Thus, the social network is the customer to win. The social media that it generates wins the customer. Scott McNealy, ex-CEO of SUN Microsystems, said, "the network is the computer." Along those lines, we believe: "the social network is the customer."

1.1.2. Social channel is the trusted consultative channel

The social network of customers can be seen as a channel between the company and the customers, as shown in figure 1.4. Messages from the company are received by the social network, which interprets, discusses and develops an opinion of the product, brand, services, events, etc., and gives customers an in-depth review. The social network is a consultative channel for the customers. It provides the added value of interpreting and advising customers about a company's products. It also amplifies the pluses and minuses of the company's messages. If your messages resonate with the social channel, this will help you to win customers, since customers trust their friends in the channel and see them as unbiased. However, the channel is brutally honest; if your messages are interpreted as misleading to the channel, customers will be forewarned.

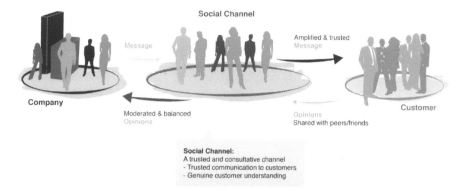

Figure 1.4: Social channel to your customers
The social network of customers can be seen as a two-way consultative channel between the company and the customers. In one direction, it provides added value in interpreting a company's messages and advising customers. In the other direction, the social channel provides the company with a genuine, integrated and balanced reading of what the customers are saying about the company.

The social channel also provides the company with a genuine, integrated and balanced reading of what customers are saying about the company. The channel balances out individual, extreme opinions, which gives you a richer understanding of your customers' opinions.

The social channel can be treated as a two-way communication channel with customers, along with other channels, such as public relations, retail and advertising, each with their own special features and benefits. Taking advantage of the social channel to create dialog with customers can be very rewarding.

1.1.3. Social network conversations: listen-understand-dialog logic-talk

Social networks provide a radically new way of communicating with customers in an ongoing dialog. It has always been the dream of all marketers to be able to hear what customers are saying, to understand them and then to talk with them about the company's offerings and benefits. Social networks make this dream come true.

Companies can also use the dialog to engage their audience in defining new products or refining existing ones. The ability to create a dialog is critical to building a relationship with the customer based on mutual understanding.

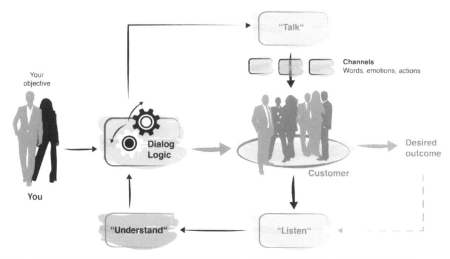

Figure 1.5: A conversation in a real-life face-to-face meeting
A conversation in a social network works the very same way as a face-to-face business conversation in an actual meeting. You pursue a desired outcome. First you (should) listen to your customer's story, situation, needs, concerns, etc. with your desired outcome in mind. In this way, you develop an understanding of your customer's position. Before you talk, you have "dialog logic" in your head. Then you talk using a combination of words, emotions, actions, show-and-tell, etc. to make a convincing proposal.

To understand how this works in a social network, let us first see how a business conversation runs in an actual, physical meeting as shown in figure 1.5. A company goes to a customer meeting with an objective (closing a deal with the customer) and there is a desired outcome in the company representative's mind (selling specific products at the best price). First you listen to the customer's story, situation, needs and concerns with your desired outcome in mind. Based on what you hear and your judgment, you develop an understanding of your customer's position. Before you make your proposal based on that understanding, you develop a plan, the "dialog logic" of how you would present your offer. Then you talk, making your proposal. The talking consists of words, emotions, actions and show-and-tell to make a convincing proposal. Then you listen again and the cycle evolves into a dialog-based conversation that, when done right, should result in your desired outcome. We will see that in a social network the communication follows a similar pattern, but uses the technologies available in social media.

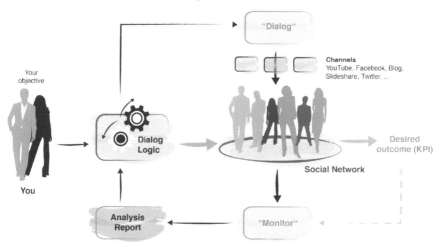

Figure 1.6: A conversation in a social network
A social network conversation is similar to a face-to-face interaction. Social media "monitoring" of a number of indicators replaces listening. Tracking and analyzing this set of indicators over time gives you an understanding of customer thinking and opinions. Based on this understanding, you develop the dialog logic of talking to the customer's social network. The dialog logic indicates which messages may resonate with the customer's social network in the current situation. This dialog is carried out with the social network via a combination of appropriate channels that communicate the right message in the right tone to the social network.

In a social network, the conversation follows the illustration in figure 1.6. Listening to the customers is replaced by social media monitoring. A number of tools, such as Radian 6 or Alterian, exist that allow you to monitor which topics members of the community discuss in the social network during any period of time. For example, if you want to monitor interest in cars, you could monitor what percentage of people talk about BMW or Audi in a given week.

You could also measure the mood or sentiment of those conversations.

You could gain insight into which features the social network considers most interesting. If you monitor the network over a year-long period, you can track social media opinion trends. This is very valuable information, especially for marketing purposes, as it allows you to generate the appropriate messages to customers. Tracking and analyzing a set of indicators over time, you develop an understanding of customers' thoughts and opinions.

There are various ways of using this very valuable social insight and understanding. One approach is to use it to improve your product or service. If the social feedback clearly indicates dissatisfaction with a product feature, that can be improved. Another way is to use this social insight to formulate messages that resonate better with the audience and can be used in a traditional media campaign and in product information.

Another option is to figure out how best to talk and engage with the audience. Using social understanding with monitoring, the company can develop an algorithm – we call it "dialog logic" – for how to engage the customer's social network. Dialog logic determines which messages are most likely to resonate with the customer's social network in a given situation. This dialog can be carried out via a combination of channels – Facebook, Twitter, YouTube, SlideShare and industry-specific blogs – that communicate the right messages with the right tone to the social network. All of this is very similar to a conversation in a face-to-face meeting. Most social media campaigns and interactions with customers take this form of listen-understand-dialog logic-talk. It is a closed loop in which the feedback from listening is a critical element. Philosophers and therapists have long counseled: "Listen, understand and think before you talk." Social media allows you to do just that in the virtual space.

1.1.4. Social media is an opinion-building platform

The quality of decision making has evolved significantly in recent decades. Social media adds a new dimension to it by enabling "opinion-based" decision making, that is, taking into account the opinions of people you trust: your friends, peers and family. Social media is also an effective platform for companies to use, to develop opinions and motivate their customers to make better decisions.

Hundreds of years ago, most decision making was based on gut feeling, or in some cases the gut feeling of a few people around you. Later, newspapers added more reliable information for making decisions. Computers, especially the Internet, now allow people to analyze much more data and information before coming to a decision. This has significantly bettered the quality of decision making because people can make fact- and information-based decisions, whether about buying a new camera, setting up a factory, selecting a hotel for a vacation, or hiring a new employee.

It is now possible to make decisions based on the collective opinions of the masses, for example, when you buy a book on Amazon or select a hotel for your vacation based on ranking and reviews. Social media platforms such as Facebook and Twitter go a step further and allow you to filter in the opinions of people you trust: your friends. Your friends can even recommend what they like and do not like, what they have tried and what they prefer. This provides a sharper focus to your decision-making and is one of the biggest gifts of social media: trusted opinion-based decision-making. This is true for business decisions, such as selecting features for your new product, and for personal decisions, such as which movie to watch tonight. Opinions include the comprehensive views of real people incorporating their varied lifestyles and experiences, making social media a far more valuable factor in decision making than facts, information or gut feeling alone. We believe that if, for example, 76% of your trusted friends on Facebook were to say that they are very happy with their iPhones, this information would be a much bigger help to you in deciding which smart phone to buy than detailed information on the various features of several different smart phones.

Summary

- Communication is a core human need born from our need to survive. Better communicators survive. Technologies that allow more effective communication have been consistently better adopted. Social media allows us to communicate more effectively in our chosen communities, using technology breakthroughs for the Internet, devices and applications.
- Social media and social networks have existed throughout history. Internet and related technologies have given the social networks global and instantaneous reach with negligible cost or effort. This gives social media new meaning and enormous value in communication, creating a wide impact in personal and business situations.
- Technologies that drive communication efficiency are in the space of available media, means of interactions, devices used to consume and create media, and infrastructure. Social media is enabled by technologies for users to generate and publish their own media (Web 2.0), interactions via social networks, mobile Internet devices and the cloud infrastructure.
- The social network that surrounds a customer is the real customer to win.
- The social channel connects companies to their customers and provides a trusted consultative path and a way of understanding what customers are thinking and saying.
- The communication dialog between the company and customers in social networks is very similar to one in a physical business meeting. Much can be learned from the communication dynamics of a face-to-face meeting.
- Social media allows more effective decision making by taking into consideration the experience-based opinions of people you know and trust: your friends, peers and family. Social media is also an effective platform for companies to develop opinions within the social network of their customers.

2. The Social Resource

This chapter covers the fundamentals of the social resource: what it is and how it can be deployed. We show how social media extends the social resource you already have and makes it much bigger, wider, global, instantaneous and mobile in access. This gives the social resource a unique potential to help you and your company in almost all business areas. Here we also explain how to use your social resource effectively by aligning it to your strategies and activating it to effectively help your business with any mission, be it hiring, product development, marketing, sales or decision-making.

In the last chapter, we looked at some fundamental concepts of social media – how it evolved, how it works and what is unique about it – especially as applied to businesses. "So what?," you may ask, "What is the real value in using it?" The simple answer is: it helps you to understand, develop and use the social resource.

We are all familiar with our social resource from our non-digital, day-to-day lives. It is common knowledge that the more people we know and regularly communicate with, the greater our advantages. Our social resource gives us a strong feeling of belonging, closeness and support. We can bounce ideas off of it, learn from it, refine our information, discover facts, brainstorm ideas, seek help, develop and fine-tune opinions, and so on. It is also mutual; our friends get the same benefits from us. It is a community of people who voluntarily stay networked and available to each other for unstructured, unplanned interactions, not knowing how, or in which situations, we may interact and help each other. We experience this every day in our personal and business lives. This is our social resource.

Our community (defined here as friends, family, peers) recommends movies to watch, books to read, supermarkets to shop in, dentists to go to, candidates to hire, job opportunities to pursue, business deals to trust, or features to build into a product. It also shares with us the insights its members have gained from their own experiences, which we, in turn, can use in our lives. There is a level of built-in trust among the members of the community that enables all of them to take these insights as authentic and valuable. We have grown up with this invaluable resource, so we take it for granted. It is tremendously useful and it makes life much easier. It is also available for free, since we do it for each other.

Of course, you pay a price for developing and maintaining the social resource. You need to invest time and effort in meeting people, talking to them, helping them, entertaining them, and offering your views on their areas of interest. Due to the time, effort and skills needed to maintain a physical relationship with the other members of your community, there is a limit to the size of your social circle, generally defined as family and close friends and business and hobby contacts. Each addition to the community requires further investment. We make this investment, and make it willingly, because there is great value in mutual belonging, support, sharing and closeness.

So, what is new about the social resource? Internet-based social media gives our social resource a tremendous boost. It allows us to significantly reduce the amount of time and effort required to maintain relationships within our communities. It is instantaneous and worldwide in reach. Through the use of smart mobile devices and cloud services, you can access it from anywhere, allowing you to stay in constant contact with your entire community. This is true for us as individuals, and also collectively for businesses. Social media-efficient employees of a company can leverage their social resource for the benefit of the company far better than in the past.

They can be actively engaged with a much larger social resource on a daily basis than before. The social resource can give a company whose employees take advantage of their own social resource a tremendous advantage over those who ignore this valuable asset. Figure 2.1 illustrates the expanding reach and size of the social resource, with newer communication technologies in all areas of life, simplified to just four areas.

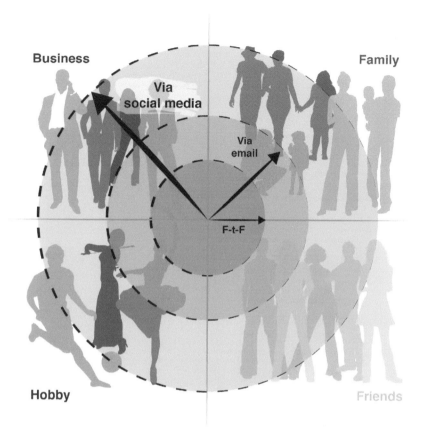

Figure 2.1: Expanding social resources
In simplified form, your social resources can be categorized broadly as friends and family and hobby and business contacts. The time and effort needed to communicate with the members of your social resource determines the size of the community you can maintain. Your social resource expands with better and faster communication technologies. Social media greatly enhances the size of your social resource and your ability to leverage it.

2.1. Let us look at some unique advantages of tapping our social resource using Internet-based social media:

2.1.1. Social resource aids fast opinion building and decision-making

- Most social media communication is asynchronous, as with SMS (i.e., text messages), in that people need not be available (i.e., online) in order to communicate with them.
- Each member of the community can be informed of the entire dialog and share what happens with any other member, giving the interactions a feeling of closeness, of "all being in the same room."
- It is possible to have group discussions and to build opinions with interested members, independent of each member's location and time zone. This feature significantly accelerates decision making for any person or organization.
- An active and involved social media dialog on a controversial topic can develop a multifaceted, balanced opinion, since each member can contribute his or her views and see all sides of a topic or product to make a more informed decision.
- One of the biggest gifts of social media is "trusted opinion-based decision making." Opinions include the comprehensive views of real people with their individual lifestyles and life experiences, making this a far more valuable factor in decision making than mere factual information or intuition. If 76% of your trusted friends on Facebook were to say that they are very happy with the event organizer they use, this would likely be a much bigger help to you in choosing an event organizer for your next function than getting detailed information about various event organizers.

- Social media is being generated, even if you do not participate. People keep "talking behind your back," even if you do not choose to engage. However, if you do engage, you have the opportunity to contribute your own opinion to the debate. More importantly, you have the ability to develop a positive social profile and social equity (a social "bank balance") to protect you from a potential negative situation.

2.1.2. Social resource dialogs are online and search ready

- The entire history of communication stays on record and can be reviewed by new members and others who could not stay connected for any reason.
- Past conversations can be searched by specific topic and theme to develop overviews and additional insights.

2.1.3. Social resource lets individuals and companies offer profiles

- Each member (friend) has a self-created profile that others can check to ascertain the background, interests, specialties and mutual contacts of any other member. This allows for the fast and easy discovery of relevant contacts.

2.1.4. Social resource filters and provides useful information

- Many people feel overwhelmed by information overload. The traditional technique of gathering information on a given subject does not work efficiently anymore due to the complexity, amount of material available, and due to a lack of time and expertise. The Internet is exploding with information and the best search engines can only help you to a certain extent.

- Social media is our protection from information overload. Your social network becomes your agent and consultant in providing experience-based recommendations to help you make decisions much faster than you would use any other method. A wide circle of chosen social media friends acts as an intelligent, like-minded filter that selects and comments on many topics of interest to you. The wider the community, the more areas it filters for you. As a result, information comes to you, rather than you having to hunt it down.

- Social media saves you a lot of time by concentrating your attention on topics that interest you. Your social network provides a filter and offers you a selection of information from sources both familiar and new, many with useful comments and opinions that may help you.

2.2. Social resource is turbo charged by the Internet

Your social resource is a network of people who are aligned with your vision and mission. You can align your social resource to your strategies and activate it to reach your goals, as shown in figure 2.2. Today's Internet-based social media tools and platforms provide unique opportunities for harnessing this resource to achieve your business goals efficiently.

Shares your vision and mission

Figure 2.2: Your social resource: a network of people who share your vision or mission
Your social resource is made up of individuals who generally share your vision and support your mission. Some are more aligned with this vision or mission than others.

An effective, well-developed and aligned social resource can be encouraged to operate on your behalf, of its own motivation, to achieve tangible business benefits for you. It can extract very useful and relevant insights for you that significantly improve the effectiveness of your decision-making.   Essentially, you can harnesses the power of your social network — its knowledge, insights, skills, capabilities, and networks — and use it for the benefit of your mission. Imagine having the best minds in the world working in your interest, driven by their own motivation, working to help you accomplish your business goals.

As we noted in the introduction, any given business has a variety of resources. These include energy, capital, expertise, intellectual property, patents, employees, partners, geographic location, technology and real estate. A successful business efficiently converts its available resources into valuable and marketable output and does so better than its competitors. The social resource is a critical new resource to add to this list. It can significantly improve a business's ability to design and manufacture products, hire better employees, use their knowledge in more innovative ways and sell more smartly than its competitors.

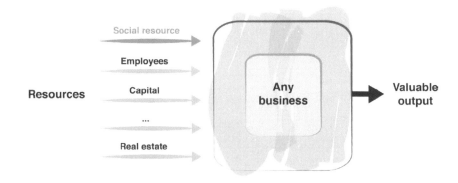

Figure 2.3: A business transforms its resources into valuable output
Any business converts its resources into valuable output to generate revenues. The social resource should be considered one such asset, along with other, more familiar ones such as capital, real estate and employees.

Most business leaders already say that their employees are their best resources. Indeed, it is through the creativity, ideas, knowhow and hard work of individual employees that most of a given company's successes are achieved. However, employees offer still more potential. Every employee has many insights and ideas on how to improve a company's products, processes, customer relationships, employee satisfaction, hiring of candidates, etc. This social resource of the company can be easily tapped into using the appropriate social media platforms and can be converted into significant benefits for both the company and its employees. Similarly, customers and consultants are the best sources of insight into which features are most needed to improve an existing product or to define a new one. Through crowd sourcing techniques, the social resource can be tapped to develop a winning product.

2.3. Winning, aligning and activating your social resource

So what is the secret strategy for building and deploying a strong, effective social resource for a business? The answer is that it requires:

- leadership by the business: transparent and open, with an engaging vision or mission
- social media expertise
- a strategic approach

The strategic approach to developing a strong, effective social resource requires three clear steps, shown in figure 2.4.

Steps	Desired impact	Synergy with social resource
1. Win	Grow your social resource by offering a shared vision or mission	Why are we in this together? (Resonance of vision)
2. Align	Align your social resource to your strategies and ways of operating	How do we operate to achieve our success (method and means)?
3. Activate	Activate your aligned social resource for a specific goal	What exactly do we want to achieve together (purpose)?

Figure 2.4: Winning, aligning and activating your social resource
To leverage your social resource, you need to win the right members (people who share your vision or mission), align it with your strategies and activate it to act on your behalf. This maps well with our WOW! methodology.

2.3.1. Step 1 - Win:

The strategic approach requires the company to have a very clear and transparent vision of what it stands for and what its values are. This vision, along with the company mission, should be easy for people to understand, relate to and aspire to. This requires true leadership in the company. The leadership must listen to and understand the people it wants to win for the social resource. It must communicate a vision and a mission that people are willing to work towards.

For ease of understanding, we will use the example of Greenpeace. This organization's vision of a clean environment is very clear and easy to understand. It resonates with many people. Its mission is also very clear: to resolve difficult environmental situations using positive energy and urgency of action.

To build your social resource, you have to win followers or friends who share your vision and mission because they are genuine fans of your product or service. Greenpeace has a huge social resource of individuals who share its vision and mission. Having "Like" or "+1" fans alone is not enough. Your social resource must be composed of genuine supporters of your vision or mission. Leadership is needed to drive your vision or mission through society to win the right members for your social resource. This is illustrated in figure 2.2. Propagating your vision and winning members on the Internet requires social media expertise.

2.3.2. Step 2 - Align:

Once you have a social resource composed of members who share your vision, you will need to align them to your strategies — how you operate, your approach, style, methods, tools and targets. Greenpeace's strategy involves a bold, direct, confrontational method of stopping environmental violations. This alignment requires business leadership and clear communication. Dell and Starbucks, which use their social resources for product innovation, have clearly outlined a methodology for the social resource to follow, illustrated in 2.5. The social resource must be aligned to this. (For a detailed description of how to develop the social resource for your company, see Chapter 4.)

You   Social resource   Your strategy
aligned to your strategy

Figure 2.5: Your social resource: aligned with your operational strategy
In order to have your social resource be of direct help to your business, it should be aligned with your strategy. That is how you get a coherent effort from all members.

2.3.3. Step 3 - Activate:

A strategy-aligned social resource that shares your vision is ready to act in support of your goals. This requires activation via social media. Activation generally requires emotional or material incentives to action. This is illustrated in figure 2.6. Clear leadership from your company as well as social media expertise play an important role in achieving success here. Greenpeace is highly effective in activating its social resource for specific actions, such as saving rainforests or protesting toxic packaging.

You

Social resource
activated for your specific goal

Your specific goal*

*Win customers, innovate, promote your product, etc...

Figure 2.6: Your social resource: activated to accomplish your goals
You have to motivate your social resource members to act and to work coherently toward achieving your specific business goal, such as participating in the development of a new product or marketing a product or an idea.

The social resource is a powerful resource only if its members share a vision, are aligned to your strategies and are properly activated (i.e., incentivized) to act toward achieving your clearly defined goals.

Summary

- As with any resource, your social resource needs to be developed, aligned and activated to be useful.
- Every business has a variety of resources. These include energy, capital, expertise, intellectual property, patents, employees, partners, geographic location, technology and real estate. A successful business efficiently converts its available resources into valuable and marketable output and does so better than its competitors. The social resource is an additional critical resource that can significantly improve your business's ability to design and manufacture superior products, hire better employees, use their knowledge in more innovative ways and sell more smartly than your competitors.
- The social resource is a community of people voluntarily networked and available to each other for unstructured, unplanned interactions. They do not know how or in which situations they may interact and help each other. This form of interaction is familiar from daily life.
- Internet-based social media gives our social resource a tremendous boost. It allows us to significantly reduce the investment of time and effort in maintaining relationships within our communities of friends and business colleagues. It is instantaneous and worldwide in reach. Through the use of smart mobile devices and cloud services, it can be accessed from anywhere – allowing users to stay in contact with their entire community anywhere, at any time. This gives it an entirely new potential to help both your business and yourself.
- In order to use your social resource to help you achieve specific business goals, you have to develop a social resource that shares your vision and mission, align it with your strategies and then motivate it to act on your goals.

3. Social Resource Generates Business Success

The social resource can materially boost your business productivity and competitiveness in a variety of areas. This chapter shows you how your social resources can be deployed in a few popular business areas, such as product development, marketing, brand building, innovation and hiring.

The social resource of a company comprises of various circles, as shown in figure 3.1. Employees, consultants, channels, partners, vendors, customers, friends and peers are all part of your social resource and, if aligned and activated, they can help you achieve business success. There are many real examples of how thousands of companies leverage their social resources to gain significant business advantage.

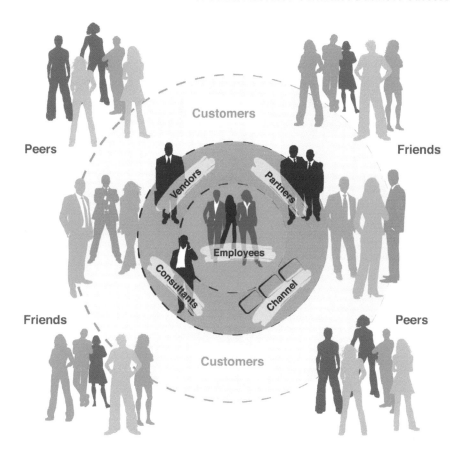

Figure 3.1: The social resource of a business

Employees are at the heart of the social resources of a company – both as contributors to and users of social resources. Consultants, partners, vendors and channels are also very significant resources. Customers themselves can become a significant social resource if engaged well. Social media lends itself very well to this engagement.

In this chapter, we want to expose you to a few areas in which the social resource is popularly deployed by businesses. This should give you an idea of the broad range of areas in which your social resources can be utilized.

1.   Product development
2.   Manufacturing
3.   Hiring
4.   Customer service
5.   Marketing campaigns
6.   Brand and image building
7.   Crisis management
8.   Innovation

3.1. Product development

The success of product development is measured in terms of lowering the costs of development, innovation and achieving high market acceptance. Most companies dedicate groups to the task of defining and developing products through the process of planning, concept, design, market research and testing. Research has shown that the best sources of ideas for product development come from customers, consultants and partners. This group is exposed to products very intimately and knows which areas to improve, which killer features to add and how to position them in the market using an external perspective of the customers and users. Employees can also contribute internal process improvement ideas. If the social resource of employees, customers, consultants and partners is aligned and activated through incentives, it can contribute amazing, out-of-the-box ideas to the internal product development team and help to boost all success indicators. This clearly requires enlightened company leadership as well as openness to working with external companies in traditionally closed areas, such as product development. You can harness the power of your established social resource not just to reduce costs, but also to make new products more innovative and better accepted by the market.

3.2. Manufacturing

The success of world-class manufacturing is measured by lower costs per unit and highest quality. This generally translates into reduced defect rates, process optimization to reduce time, raw materials utilization, labor skills and costs, etc. The manufacturing department is responsible for managing these particular indicators of success. The employees involved in manufacturing, the vendors of equipment and the raw material suppliers form a part of your social resource that has very practical insights into and instincts about many of the manufacturing parameters. If open interaction and discussion is enabled in the social network, with incentives to improve manufacturing, the social resource would be in the best position to come up with solutions to improve the indicators through crowd sourcing. The social resource has the most accurate insights, the motivation to improve and excel, the will to collaborate and the incentives to develop the best solutions rapidly. Even here, enlightened company leadership is required, as is openness to working with employees and external companies. However, you can harness the power of your established social resource to reduce costs and to motivate your employees to contribute in a unique way.

3.3. Hiring

Hiring the right people is one of the keys to business success and is always a challenge. Improper hiring can take a huge toll on the morale and efficiency of a group. Professional headhunters are expensive and the hiring process is lengthy. If you can, instead, tap your social resource for suitable candidates, you are likely to find more suitable leads faster because your social resource knows your company, environment and requirements. Social media has become a very common resource both for job hunting and recruitment. It is fast, efficient and costs little.

3.4. Customer service

Great customer service creates customer loyalty. It is one of the most important considerations for ensuring repeat buyers. Customers want speedy access, accurate answers and hassle-free, fast resolution. Customers are often the best social resource for helping other customers who use social media. Customers who have resolved a service issue can be aligned, activated and incentivized to help other customers with a similar situation. Your service employees should also be a part of your social resource, actively helping customers who post a service issue on social networks or on your fan page. Such proactive help is highly appreciated. Customer help desks can be set up as part of a social media site on which customers with problems can interact with customers who are incentivized to help.

3.5. Marketing campaigns

Satisfied customers and fans of your products are your evangelists. This group forms a very effective social resource that can talk about your products and spread the word in their networks. Many campaigns activate these fans to write about a product and their personal experiences with it in their posts. By doing so, they essentially are marketing for you, working from their own conviction and passion. They are also far more credible and effective since they are unbiased but also known to their circle of friends. This is a very convincing word-of-mouth recommendation technique. Cultivating, aligning and activating the social resource of your satisfied customers and fans can be a very rewarding program.

3.6. Brand and image building

The fans who are aligned with your vision are your best brand ambassadors. Many top brands, such as BMW, Apple, and Nike, have significant branding programs. They have a social resource of millions of fans who express positive emotions about their brands of choice in their social networks. The same is true for celebrities, sports figures and businesses. Each has a huge social resource of fans who spontaneously express and maintain the brand image. These entities and individuals invest great effort in creating and sustaining a personal dialog with their social resources to maintain a strong relationship and ensure alignment.

3.7. Crisis management

Crises happen without warning. The consequences of a crisis can also catch you by surprise. In business, crises can come in the form of a branding scandal, production crash, product recall – or worse. In a crisis, you need help in areas in which you may not have all the necessary expertise. This is where your social resource really comes in handy. A sizable and active social resource is likely to have the skills – individually or collectively – to help you generate outside-the-box solutions to contain and resolve the crisis swiftly. Since crises often happen unannounced, you need a social resource that is developed and aligned so it can swing into action when needed. Many "freelance" members may also join your social resource out of a human urge to help in crisis, as is commonly seen in natural calamities. You need to be in a position to communicate with these individuals and use their help in a crisis.

3.8. Innovation

Innovation is one of the most unusual and creative human abilities: figuring out a new way of doing things. One characteristic of innovation is that it cannot be planned. The eureka moment just happens – when, how and to whom, cannot be foreseen. What is known is that certain environments foster and accelerate innovation. A tension-free environment, in which discussions among a diverse group of people can occur openly and spontaneously – as in coffee houses of the past – makes it more likely for people to arrive at innovative breakthroughs. Researchers attribute this to the way the brain works. When someone has a hunch about something and expresses it, then combines it with hunches from others in an open discussion and these suddenly click in someone else's brain as a complete idea or solution, the result is a breakthrough innovation. Social media is the new virtual coffee house. It is here that hunches are openly, constantly being exchanged, fostering innovation. A healthy social resource that is aligned and motivated for open discussions, allows innovation to be seeded and bear fruit. Unlike a coffee house, the geographical and cultural diversity possible in social networks is unlimited and the right combination of hunches – like the right combination of pieces of a jigsaw puzzle – can fall into place faster in the brain of any member of your social resource.

We intended this chapter to provide you with an overview of the versatility and power of the aligned social resource in helping you in almost all areas of business. Like any other resource, you must cultivate, align and use it to your advantage. Chapter 4 describes in detail the key buildings blocks for developing your social resource. This is the core of the social media expertise needed to leverage your social resource. Chapter 5 will then describe in detail a few business applications and how they are constructed using the building blocks. We hope to illustrate how it all comes together and the benefits that result when the social resource is applied to a concrete business practice.

Summary

- The social resource can be used to improve almost all areas of your business operation.
- The most popular areas are marketing, branding, hiring and product development.
- Crowd sourcing and social media monitoring are popular methods of tapping into the social resource.

4. Building Blocks to Develop the Social Resource for your Company

To develop the social resource for your company, you need to understand and master the basic building blocks. In this chapter, we explain and present the underlying concepts and ideas. We will look at the social network and how it works, how to engage to win people, how to share things that matter, how to listen to and learn from people, search and be found, develop services that multiply, get close to your customer, engage in commerce and activate users.

Rome was not built in a day. Neither was the Internet, nor the social resource. When iron was mined or oil was discovered and put to use, it took years to understand how to optimize the processes needed to use it well and to maximize its benefits. Just because social media has evolved so swiftly, does not make "going social" a switch you simply turn on and watch the benefits flow. Social media has been a revolution for individuals. Now companies need to respond to it. Social media is more of an evolution than a revolution for business. As the possibilities are just opening up, so are the numbers of people using the social resource to their advantage. There is much to be learned, discovered, advanced and created. If you as a business owner do not take the time to get it right, the benefits will not come. In fact, you may be disappointed and are likely to be surpassed by the individuals and organizations that do get it right.

Imagine you are a kid who loves to play soccer and dreams of becoming a top player. What can you do to realize this dream? It is not easy to know where to start. Do you have passion and are you willing to work hard? Most top players are passionate about their sport. Find the right team and the right coach, meet the right people to support you and, essentially, take advantage of the opportunities that come your way. Eventually you may become a top league player.

So it is with tapping the social resource. The beginning is not easy, the path may be unclear and you may not know who can help you. However, it is possible to discover the right way, if you are dedicated to finding it. We can make your task easier by showing you a clear path to developing your social resource.

In this chapter, we focus on the basic building blocks you must understand and master in order to develop your company's social resource. Developing your social resource is a critical first step on the road to social media success for your business. As the social resource is a new and growing phenomenon, it is important to understand the concepts that support it. The technologies associated with social media will change. The channels and methods will also change, as creative people find new ways to leverage the social resource. But the underlying building blocks will remain the basis for your decisions in taking direction and starting to move along the road to success.

Here are the ten fundamental social media building blocks we have identified:

1.   The social network – our social foundation
2.   Profile and dialog – reaching out to win people
3.   Channels – the right place for your social media interactions
4.   Content – sharing what matters
5.   Monitoring and measuring – listening to and learning from people
6.   Advertising and search – searching and being found
7.   Social apps – services that multiply
8.   Social CRM – always be with your customer
9.   Commerce – using the social currency
10. Campaigns – activate your users

4.1. The social network - our social foundation

The concept: The social network allows you to connect with people and businesses, to have a dialog, to share and spread information and services globally, anytime and anywhere.

The business impact: You can leverage a free, global, efficient, real-time communication and collaboration infrastructure with your target audience, customers, partners and employees.

4.1.1. The social network

The social network is the fundamental infrastructure for social media. It is the backbone of communication and interaction among people. Understanding how it works is essential in developing and using the social resource. The social network combines the web-like infrastructure of the Internet with the communication capabilities of the telephone. It connects people and businesses on a global scale, anywhere, on any device, in real time. It also has a built-in memory that allows users to record all interactions, and these can later be searched. The social network is the foundation of the social revolution.

Your social network starts with you as a person. Just as in real life, your social profile defines your identity: how you look, act and interact socially, as well as what you like and say. People want their social profiles to look good; they know social media is an open stage. Other people form their opinions and expectations of you based on your social profile and your social interactions. To some, you might be a likable, intelligent and trustworthy person, while to others you might seem boring or irrelevant. Just as in real life, these impressions are very subjective, and it is important to note that you cannot be everything to everybody.

4.1.2. Your friends, followers and fans

The people watching you and interacting with you are called your "social friends," your followers, or fans. They decide whether or not to interact with you and they have different expectations for watching and interacting with you. The term "friend" is quite misleading here. In social networks, you interact with people in many different ways and each interaction has its unique context. There may be a family member who needs help, a relative who wants to ask a question, a good friend who offers useful advice, a neighbor who is looking for small talk, a colleague who wants help, or a customer giving you valuable advice. Independent of your relationship, your interaction may turn out to be useful, sometimes even groundbreaking or, conversely, boring and irrelevant. You know this from real life and have found ways to manage it efficiently. This is your social network.

Customer

Figure 4.1: Your connection to your friends in the social network
In the social network, you can directly connect with people to have a conversation. You can talk to them and listen to what they have to say.

The global social network consists of varying levels of connectedness, starting with you and your direct contacts, and moving out to further degrees of connection, like your friend's friends, and their friends. We believe that moving away from your known contacts can be very rewarding in spawning out-of-the box ideas, and even inspiring, as you interact with new people. However, as you move out further into the network, you loose the social trust factor, unless you consider the people you find there to be experts.

The first level – direct relationships

The first level of your social network is defined by your direct relationships with your friends and followers. These are people you know in real life or have met though social media. You have a direct connection with them. The quality of your relationship with them is described as your "social capital" with them and this can vary significantly among the people you know personally and the people you meet digitally. You are likely to have the greatest social capital with your family members and close friends, as they are likely to exert the greatest effort in doing things that provide the highest value for you. In most platforms, you can see the first level of your social network in your friend, follower or fan list. With this level, you share an infrastructure to follow, interact and communicate with your relationships, independent of time and place, on a global scale. This is called your "social graph." You can exchange messages, ideas, photos, friends, locations and many other things with your first level network. In return they can comment, "like," share and spread your communication. Doing so has a direct impact on your social capital, which may increase if your communication is valuable or decrease over time based on your actions and interactions, both in the real world and in the social network.

The second level – the ripple effect

The second level of your social network is your friend's friends and their connections. If you are, for example, in a dialog with a good friend, all of your first level friends can listen in and interact. In addition, your friend's first level of friends can also listen in and interact. If both you and your friend have 150 friends each, this communication is followed by your combined 300 friends. Potentially, they can all follow this communication and interact. And these 300 have their own friends. So if all these friends also interact, theoretically an additional 45,000 friends could follow the conversation and interact, should everyone engage. However, in most conversations only a few people join the discussion. Whether people engage and how much they engage, depends on how much social capital you have with them, how aligned they are and/or simply how interesting the topic is to them at that given moment. This is called the ripple effect. Welcome to the power of the social network.

During the emergency landing of a plane on the Hudson River in New York City in 2009, more than a million people watched and interacted on the topic using Twitter. Millions of people followed and discussed the revolt against the authoritarian governments in Egypt and the Middle East. Of course, the social network consists of many individual sites and services, and not all are open and compatible. However, they are all somewhat interconnected and can relay information and interactions among them across the globe.

Customer

Figure 4.2: Your friend's friends - the second-degree network.
In the social network, your friends and followers also have their own friends and followers. If your friends participate in a conversation with you, their friends can also join the conversation and spread the dialog.

4.1.3. Social Influencers

Some people have more friends, followers and fans as well as more social capital than others. These people are commonly called "social influencers," as shown in figure 4.3. Because they are watched by, trusted by and interact with a significant number of people, their communication and interactions can be quite influential. Working with influencers to spread a given message is a common social networking technique for seeding opinions. However, this only works if the messages and interactions are authentic, trustworthy and relevant, as well as aligned with the interests of the followers. A consumer goods business innovator offering financial advice might not motivate his followers to act. He will need a lot of social capital with his followers. In fact, if he talks about too many irrelevant topics, he will likely lose his following and his social capital and friends may "un-friend" him in the long run. Influencers are usually aware of their large following and are interested in maintaining it, as well as expanding their social capital. They are quite careful about how and what they communicate to their audiences.

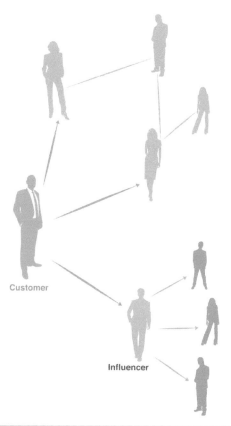

Figure 4.3: Your connection to influencers (people with many friends)
If you connect with social influencers relevant to your topics, they can help spread your conversations through the social network.

Influencers can be identified through social media monitoring. To win them, you must identify mutual interests and partner with them. Do not try to buy them in social media or ask them to do things that do not come naturally to them. This can backfire, as your influencers may publicly reveal your intentions. It is better to find a win-win situation. Of course, the customer should also win.

Practical Tip: When developing your social network, try not to focus on achieving a huge reach fast. Engagement and the ability to activate people are critical to your success. Continually test your engagement and ability to activate your audience. If you are not successful, you are likely reaching the wrong audience and need to change your acquisition strategy.

4.1.4. Companies and brands

Companies and brands are also part of the social network, as shown in figure 4.4. They have their own presence, just as individuals do. You can follow Nike or become friends with BMW. Like individuals, companies have profile pages and social interactions and can cultivate social capital. In fact, some have a great deal of social capital. Certain social platforms, like Facebook, have special technical features that enable additional functions for companies. These include providing statistics, offering more ways to present information and engage in dialog, and allowing more than one person or team to manage the profile and social interactions. The basic concept of making friends and following, as well as the social interactions themselves, are very similar.

People typically choose to make friends with and follow brands on their own because they get a product-related service or other incentives to do so. However, it is important to understand that people are well aware of the presence of companies and their objectives in social media. Once engaged in social media, companies can provide additional services to their friends and followers. For example, the German airline Lufthansa publishes flight information to people who follow its social profile. The airline can interact with its customers to make flight change recommendations if a flight is late. This interaction can be commented on and spread by the users, multiplying the service to others. This creates efficiency and reach for companies. We recommend that you work to increase your social capital and align your friends and followers in order to boost your social horsepower and enable you to leverage your social resources in the future.

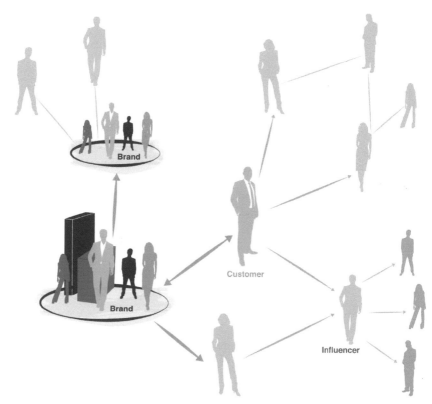

Figure 4.4: Brands in the social network
People can become friends with brands in social media, allowing the brands to "have a conversation" with their audiences. This provides additional levels of service and creates a value-added relationship.

Much discussion is focused on mixing personal and work social profiles, as the interests of people connecting to this profile vary greatly. There are many ways to address this; choosing the path that works best is an individual decision. You can create separate profiles, or use features for separating communication via lists or circles, or other means under development to address this important issue. Any of these approaches takes considerable effort, so you have to decide whether it is worthwhile. Younger people do not seem to care about this issue. They feel a blending of work and private life is natural. It is up to you to decide.

Practical Tip: When brands communicate through social media, they should indicate who is talking. People appreciate knowing they are communicating with people. This can easily be done by adding the name of the author of each post.

Companies can also engage with other companies. This is an interesting solution for working with partners. Here is a simple example: A company organizing a ski event can publish its program and information on the ski resort's profile page to attract people interacting with that ski resort, creating a win-win situation and achieving a broad reach of people interested in both skiing and that resort. In this way, both audiences can interact and benefit.

Companies can also use social networks to engage, inform and provide services to their employees. Some companies have created their own internal social networks and the big social sites have created closed groups for special target audiences, allowing them to interact in a controlled environment. Services such as Yammer and Flowr are a few of the social sites that focus on a company's internal communications. They allow employees to setup business profiles, share information, communicate, like and share content and conversation.

Technically speaking, the social network is built on the IP-based Internet infrastructure, which is commonly available in all locations and on a wide range of devices, with a communication and interaction layer on top, as well as a memory of what users do and say.

The business benefit of the social network is that it gives you a global real-time network through which to connect with your employees, partners and customers — without shouldering the direct cost associated with it. We will look at how to use this social network for your business in the following sections.

4.2. Profile and Dialog – reaching out to win people

The concept: You can convince and activate people by engaging the social network in dialog.

The business impact: Broaden your reach and increase your social capital by winning people to use their social capital in your favor.

4.2.1. Profile

Who you are is defined in part by how you look, what you communicate and what you do. Say, for instance, you meet a seasoned professional who is nicely dressed, well mannered and intelligent looking. However, when you talk with him he giggles, moves awkwardly and never looks you in the eye. Would you trust him? Would you be interested in maintaining an ongoing dialog with him? Well, it depends. Over time, people have perfected their abilities to judge other people based on appearance and actions. People build relationships and form their expectations based on watching, interacting and communicating with other people over time.

In the Internet-based social network, the first impression you make on others is your "social profile" picture, as well as your profile page. Do you know this person in real life? Is this person friendly? Is he interesting? What are the topics and conversations on his profile page? People look into the person's past conversations and social actions, "listening" to what he has to say. How does the person comment, what are his interests and concerns, who is he connected with, which pictures does he show, like and comment on? Who are his friends?

In the social network, we learn to assess this "social history" and what to expect from this person. Entering into a dialog reveals how this person thinks and acts. This completes the picture and forms the foundation for our relationship with this person in the social network. The person is awarded social capital on the basis of this information. Using this, we decide how to interact, what to comment on and how we might help this person. Since our judging processes are less precise in the social network than they are in real life, people typically react in one of two ways: they are either very wary of or far more open with strangers than they would be in real life because they unconsciously consider their interactions in the social network to be "not real," a game. This aspect makes people more likely to lie as well.

The social network provides additional features that are not readily available in the real world. On many platforms, you get direct access to an individual's social history in social networking. What has this person done and said in the past? Where has he been? Also, you can listen to conversations between people, even if you were not involved. This can reveal aspects of a person's character that you were not aware of or would not have suspected. The reason is often very simple: These people had not thought that this aspect of their character would be relevant to you, so they had not discussed it with you in real life. Personal experience shows that you can be friends with a person for more than 20 years and then, through social media, discover aspects of this person's character you had never known. In our view, this is good because it provides a complete picture of an individual and may alter the foundation for your relationship with this person. The social capital for people you know in real life is based on your interactions and experiences in both the real and the virtual worlds.

A lot has been written about the need to be authentic and build a solid reputation in social media. This only reflects the human aspect of the media and the correlation to real-world relationships and interactions. Building a successful social profile and social capital is a process you should plan well. It is mainly defined by your actions and conversations in the social network, in addition to what you do and say in real life.

Practical Tip: When engaging in social media, be yourself and focus on your strengths. Social media is a transparency machine that brings the truth to light. If you make false claims, the social network will likely discover this and you may loose all credibility. Do not use business language, use conversational language.

Companies also have profiles in the social network. A company profile is very similar to a personal profile; it is also represented by a profile picture and a profile page. The conversation, actions and stories define the social profile of the company. Some social media platforms, such as Facebook, YouTube, SlideShare and LinkedIn offer special features like analytics, adding special pages, advertising for companies, who, in return, pay money or in some way make the network more visible and valuable to its user base.

4.2.2. Dialog

One of the key concepts of the social network is the "social dialog." Without dialog, the network would likely be far less useful and would not have grown as fast as it has in recent years. Dialog among people (and with companies) is what drives social networking. It helps develop social capital, alignment between individuals and between people and businesses, and it is used to activate the social resource. Before you engage in dialog, you should listen to your social resource. Then, if you have something meaningful to say, you should engage and dialog will follow.

Figure 4.5: Dialog in social media
Example of dialog initiated by a company. Users quickly add their opinions and comments to the dialog to engage with the company and other friends.

Practical Tip: Pictures, links, albums and videos are visual means of attracting attention in the dialog. As social networks and dialog grow, it is important to use visual measures to stand out from the crowd. Visual media is also easier to consume and can be used to communicate additional information.

Dialog is also the way to spread messages through the social network, as shown in figure 4.6. The basic mechanism is simple: One person posing a question can be answered by a number of his friends. The individual's friends can also see the question and add their answers and opinions, if relevant. If the question is interesting to the network, hundreds of people may answer, comment on, share and discuss it. In that sense, the question becomes a social object, a reason for the interaction.

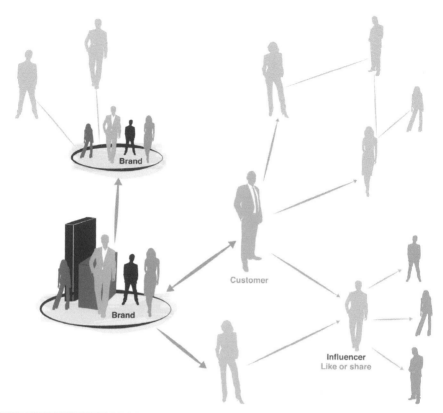

Figure 4.6: Dialog is spread through the social network based on comments or sharing
Users who participate in, like or share a conversation are making this conversation available to their friends and followers, thus potentially widening the audience for the conversation.

Dialog is essential for expanding your reach and influence in social networking. Having people comment, like, and/or share your message helps to spread the dialog throughout the social network, as the friend's friends see the expanded conversation. For some people, it is easier to engage in written dialog in the social network than it is for others. Typing on a small smart phone screen can be tedious, uncertainties about who is reading the dialog and lack of time are a few of the reasons people do not engage in written social media dialog. Social sites have been creative in addressing this. Twitter offers a re-tweet button that sends a user's existing dialog to the network of the user's friends. Instead of writing "Dear network, you should read this interesting article, which I have found on this website," users just push one button and the dialog spreads to their friends and followers. Facebook has taken this concept a step further and offers the "like it" button, which, when clicked, shows your network what you like and helps spread the message in dialog form. A "like it" button gives the dialog a positive spin. The button also provides a mechanism through which to spread social interactions to the rest of the Internet, beyond Facebook. By integrating the "like it" button into a website, people can like the website outside of Facebook and spread the link through their network, recommending it unobtrusively.

Sites like Foursquare have taken this concept of spreading dialog into the real world. The service allows you to "check in" to a location with the click of a button. Relying on smart phones with GPS capabilities, Foursquare identifies where you are and associates a location with your current position. It also allows you to add a location, if it is not yet on the network. Pushing the check-in button sends a dialog to your social network, telling them where you are. This can be commented on, liked and spread through the social network, when people value this information. This removes the burden of typing long texts and is a very effective way to initiate a dialog. Google+ has added relevance to the search results with its "+1" button, thus increasing the impact of the dialog to search results. Pressing the "+1" button posts the link of the current page to your social network and increases the search rank of this page.

Some social platforms reward their users for being active by giving them little incentives, such as virtual badges ("you are a rock star," "you are a frequent traveler") for their activities. The intention is to motivate users to frequent the site, use the service and enjoy these playful incentives, which are sometimes coupled with real life benefits. Because users perceive themselves as being on a stage in social media, these incentives work. This process, called "gamification," adds an element of fun to the interaction. When used creatively, gamification can be successful across all audiences.

Photos and videos are making big inroads into the social networks. These can also be seen as a form of dialog. Photos can easily be shared with a click. They are very popular with users, because they are fun to look at and communicate a lot of information and emotion. For example, we can write to our social networks that we are in Austria, the weather is nice, the mountains are still covered with snow and we are in a beautiful and peaceful environment. Taking and sharing a single photo communicates this and much more with far less effort. Photos and videos are a good way to initiate a dialog and are often liked and commented on. We believe they will remain an important and integral part of social communication in the future.

Let's look at a simple example of a social dialog. Let's say we are visiting Apple's World Wide Developer Conference in San Francisco. Opening the Foursquare app on the smart phone, determines that we are in the Moscone Center and offers the option to check in. Doing so and adding the optional text "Looking for new business apps", sends a message to the user's social network. The message "Just checked in (with 50 other persons) to the Moscone Center looking for business apps" is spread to Facebook and Twitter accounts (if they are linked) and is seen on the average by more than 600 friends on both platforms. Perhaps 10 of these friends like the message and five write a comment saying they are also planning to attend or have a tip for a good business app at the show. The simple check-in dialog spreads through the social networks and activates people to interact. People might decide to go to the show based on the dialog. People discuss the presentations, meet and exchange tips, just to name a few examples of the effects of one person's simple check in.

In addition, you might get direct personal value by initiating such a dialog. You could get a conference badge from Foursquare for checking into five conference locations in one month. You could get a message from the conference center that there is a special offer for attending breakout sessions. You could see which of your friends are also in the location, which influencers are there as well as easily connect and meet with them.

Practical tip: You can encourage dialog by asking questions, encouraging people to add mission information or voice their opinions and by making controversial statements. Make it easy for people to engage in dialog even on your website by adding a like it button and a social comment box.

One of the most fascinating concepts in social networking is that people naturally gravitate to communities of interest. With companies, this often happens around their products and services, where people discuss experiences and opinions. Independent of whether a company participates or not, its customers discuss the products at great length and in detail in their social networks. We are seeing the increasing importance of this effect on purchasing decisions because communication in the social network is often with trusted people, whose experiences matter in forming an opinion about a product.

This opinion formation can also happen in real time and for a single occasion, purely based on sharing a dialog. People watching the World Wide Developer Conference from anywhere in the world can talk about this event with their friends on social media. Many people do so before, during and after the show. In the social network, the communication could be searched and grouped into an ad-hoc communication channel. And the entire dialog can be viewed in this channel. This is very useful as it shows the wide range of issues, topics and insights being discussed on a given topic. These ad-hoc topics are great for watching and developing an opinion; many people use this method of tapping into the social network on a specific topic. Of course, you can plant your own dialog in these ad-hoc channels. In fact, you can directly address any or all the people searching for this topic in your communication. Because all these individuals share a common interest, you can win them if you make yourself relevant to them and their interests. This makes communicating on topics of interest a good way to increase your following.

Practical tip: You can create a channel of interest around your product or service by creating a specific channel for it, seeding the topic in social media or running campaigns to encourage people to have a dialog about it. This allows you to engage. However, you should not just sell: focus on adding value to the conversation and be authentic.

To develop your social resource, dialog is a key factor in establishing your presence and trustworthiness. The more people who participate in your conversations, the more likely they are to become friends with and follow you. If you are relevant, they will carry you through their network and talk about and recommend you to their friends. Once you build up enough social capital and once they are aligned, they will help you when you are in trouble and give you valuable feedback when needed. They will help you develop products and deliver customer service; they will, in fact, become part of your business operations.

For a company, it is important to identify the people that have a dialog with the customer. People can sense authentic dialog and they expect companies to be forthright and service oriented. They also expect quick responses. You should be careful and ensure people engaging in dialog for your company are authentic, competent and can represent the positive aspects of your corporate culture.

The business value of dialog in social media is that it allows a direct interaction with your target audience. Moreover, people engaging in dialog with you helps spread your message.

4.3. Channels – the right place for your social media interactions

The concept: In the heterogeneous global social network, there are trusted places where your target audience is active and there are services your audience appreciates and is likely to use.

The business impact: Gain efficiency and quick reach by engaging in places where your audience is and activate them through services they appreciate and find value in.

4.3.1. Channels Overview

The social network is more of an abstract layer than a real physical network. Based on the global Internet infrastructure, social platforms and services have evolved and connected, and these, in sum, make up the social network. Individual social platforms and services are often called "social channels" and have established their own way of doing things based on their own technical implementation. However, they are often interconnected; information and dialog can flow from one channel into another. Facebook, Twitter, LinkedIn, YouTube, Google+ are the most popular social channels. There are thousands of other channels available and these are constantly evolving. Often, they are focused on addressing certain audiences or delivering specific services to their users. A good overview of the plethora of social channels is presented in the conversation prism by Brian Solis (www.theconversationprism.com). It depicts the common social channels and groups them into areas for listening, learning and sharing. The prism can be used to identify relevant channels.

Practical tip: You can use social media monitoring to identify the relevant social channels for your audience by listening to the conversations and analyzing the topics of conversation. It is often more effective to go to places where conversations about a topic are happening than to try to create a new topic in channels.

Let us look at some of the most important channels from a business perspective, their main audience and purpose, as well as some of their strengths, weaknesses, opportunities and threats. Note that all of these networks are free to use and global in reach, and the barriers to entry are very low.

4.3.2. Facebook (www.facebook.com)

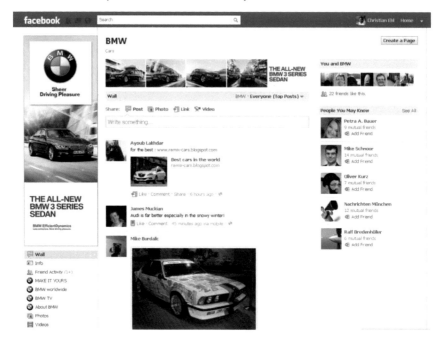

Figure 4.7: Facebook - "The social network"
Facebook is characterized by the wall, a web page that shows the dialog between the people and brands that you are connected with as well as their friends and followers. It is easy to directly engage in the conversation by pressing the like button, sharing or adding a comment.

Characteristics:
Facebook is used by more than 800 million people around the world (source: www.facebook.com/press). It offers simple conversation and sharing services. You are most likely to find your friends, family and business colleagues there. The "like" button makes it unique and helped it spread throughout the Internet, the mobile phones and beyond. Thanks to its good profiling and viral spread, it is also attractive to companies and advertisers, who fuel its financial success.

Business use:
Fan pages are good social profiles and enable effective social dialog
Helpful for developing long-term relationship with the users
Provides a timeline for a thorough brand experience
Effective targeting for efficient advertising

Strengths:	Opportunities:
Intuitive	To become the de facto standard for social networking
Most of your friends are there	To become the platform on which most developers offer social services and apps
Available on all devices	
Good profiling	
Allows signing-in to other sites with your Facebook login	To become the home of a plethora of new communities such as sports clubs, companies, musicians, where people exchange communication and dialog
Provides an open programming interface to allow developers to build applications and access social data	
Weaknesses:	**Threats:**
Ambiguous and hard-to-configure privacy settings	Lose supporters if perceived as misusing data and/or unsafe
Cluttered user interface with many features and functions	Not innovating rapidly enough in a fast- moving space (Google+ Circles, Hangout, ...)
Weak search for information, dialog and people outside of your direct network	User streams become too cluttered with irrelevant information

Table 4.2: Facebook analysis

Practical tip: We recommend that you make Facebook part of your social channel mix in the next 12 months. Its large reach and good dialog features, as well as its good integration with websites and social apps, facilitate engagement with your customers.

4.3.3. Twitter (www.twitter.com)

Figure 4.8: Twitter - open sharing with just 140 characters
Twitter allows you to share 140 character-long dialogs with your friends
and offers fast and simple interaction mechanisms both through the web
browser and on a plethora of desktop and mobile devices

Characteristics:
Twitter is unique in its ease of use, speed and simplicity. By allowing only 140- character messages, it is easy to read and spurs creativity. It is used by 120 million people (source: business.twitter.com/basics) and is often used to share news of any kind. It is the world's largest real-time knowledge database. It reveals what people are concerned with, doing, thinking and discovering right now.

Business use:
Informing and communicating with your customers (customer services)
Spotting customers and prospects (open) and interacting with them
Spreading your messages easily to broad audiences

Strengths:	**Opportunities:**
Open by nature, allows reading anything by everyone, discovering new ideas and concepts easily	Due to its open nature, it has little privacy concern and can be used as the standard for sharing open information and dialog
Simple to use, good usability and effective in communication	Open API means it can be used for man-to-machine or machine-to-machine communication
Tagging through the use of the "#" hashtag easily gives context and creates topics to read and follow	
Open API with thousands of apps	
Great for information feeds (entertainment, new, events, locations, sports), following topics	
Twitter is real time	
Weaknesses:	**Threats:**
Twitter is text-centered; you need to click on links for rich media	People wandering off to Facebook, Google+ and other networks for more multimedia features
Creative 140-character wording is sometimes hard for non-Twitterers	Never becomes mainstream because of site-specific language and navigation challenges
Information streams can be overwhelming	

Table 4.3: Twitter analysis

Practical tip: Engage in Twitter to identify trends as well as search for people engaging on a given topic.

4.3.4. Google+ (plus.google.com)

Figure 4.9: Google+ is the newest major social network

Google + allows you to sort your stream by circles (i.e., groups of interest) and offers the ability to engage in media-rich real-time conversation through its hangouts. The +1 button is relevant for search engine marketing.

Characteristics:

Google+ is the youngest major social network. It adds new concepts, such as dividing your friends into groups (circles), enabling multimedia group communication (hangouts) as well as providing good integration with Internet content through search. Google+ information increases search relevance so that if articles are "+1"ed, they can be found more easily. Another way to look at Google+ is that Google is integrating all of its numerous, diverse Internet services into a single platform.

Business use:

Spread information to a defined user group in a social way (partners, customers, prospects, employees)

Strengths:	Opportunities:
Simple and clean user interface and good overall user experience Good integration of all the Google products Unique concepts such as "circles" and "hangout" Good way to distribute media to a defined circle of people +1 is relevant to search results, supporting search marketing	Good implementation and privacy settings allow it to gain users from other social sites Establishing social media for business by having the right positioning Ability to leverage a large number of Google product customers to try out Google+ with targeted unique advantages
Weaknesses:	**Threats:**
Due to its newness, it has fewer users, and few of your contacts are likely yet on it, so it is hard to connect with all your friends A late-comer to the game of social networking, where migration to a new network means a lot of effort for those already on another platform	Innovative features are copied by other networks, which might reduce potential users' urge to migrate to Google+

Table 4.3: Google+ analysis

4.3.5. LinkedIn (www.linkedin.com)

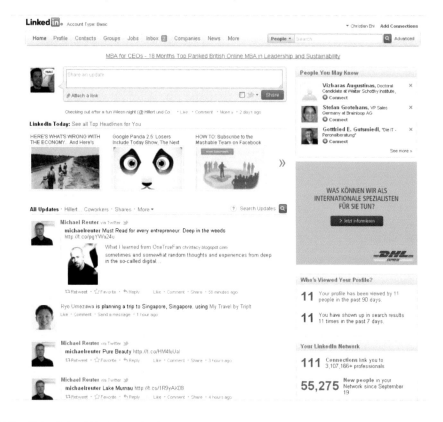

Figure 4.10: LinkedIn - the business network
LinkedIn can be used to find jobs, people and business opportunities recommended by anyone in your contact network. Employers can list jobs and search for candidates.

Characteristics:	
With more than 135 million socially networked people (source: press.linkedin.com/about), LinkedIn is a heavyweight in business communication and networking. It is a network with a business focus and positioning.	
Business use:	
Finding the right people to hire Staying in touch with your customers and partners	
Strengths:	**Opportunities:**
Good tools for business, like references, job searching, company pages	Bring social networking to business by offering campaign infrastructure and services for the business world
Weaknesses:	**Threats:**
Generally considered not very intuitive No easy consolidation between private and business lives	Business networking is moving where the customers are: Facebook, Twitter, Google+

Table 4.4: LinkedIn – the business interconnect platform

4.3.6. YouTube (www.youtube.com)

Figure 4.11: YouTube – the video platform
YouTube allows you to view popular videos on the Internet, sorted by genre, users or channels.

Characteristics:
YouTube's success is based on short videos that are easy to search discover, forward, post and view on all devices. Videos cover all possible areas of personal and business interest. 48 hours of videos are uploaded every minute and three billion videos are viewed per day. YouTube has become so popular that it has become the second-largest search engine as people look for video content of all kinds: entertainment, sports, how-to guides, product information, etc. (Source: http://www.youtube.com/t/press_statistics)

Business use:
Provide emotional product videos, tests, testimonials, reviews
Explain products and their usage, as well as the thinking behind the products
Provide value-added information around products and services

Strengths:	Opportunities:
Enables video communication on all devices	Video becomes the language of communication as it becomes even easier to create and upload videos
Provides global content from all areas of life	
Highly liked and used because video content is easy to digest	
Good integration into other sites	
Weaknesses:	**Threats:**
Few social features make it hard to interact, comment and spread	Copyright infringements force YouTube to continuously take down content
	Social video features are integrated into all the social sites, taking away traffic from YouTube

Table 4.5: YouTube - the largest video social platform

Practical Tip: Upload short how-to videos about your products and services that can be found and embedded in dialog. Videos are a great and easy way of explaining things and motivating people emotionally.

4.3.7. SlideShare (www.slideshare.com)

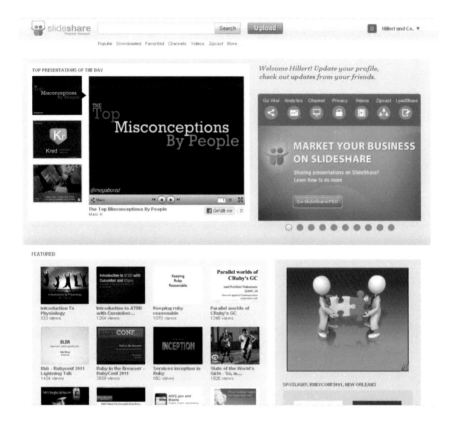

Figure 4.12: SlideShare - the presentation network
SlideShare shows popular presentations by category, topics, users and channels. Users can easily flip through presentations and contact the authors.

Characteristics:
SlideShare is a network focused on communicating through presentations. With more than 55 million monthly visitors (source: www.slideshare.net/tour), SlideShare has become the place for visual presentation communications and easy knowledge transfer. Presentations are easy to view and flip through. Sharing and commenting features enable popular social dialog.

Business use:
Show your knowledge and competence
Direct interactions with people watching presentations
Discover and hire knowledge owners and good communicators

Strengths:	**Opportunities:**
Largest presentation exchange platform	Visual communication becomes mainstream and presentations are the key element to delivering them because they are easy to create and fun and informative to watch
Presenting the world of good presentations and online meetings	
Easy-to-use, flip-through multimedia presentations	
Great pool of knowledge and inspiration on business topics	
Weakness:	**Threats:**
Relatively unknown	People may tire of too many dull presentations

Table 4.6: SlideShare analysis

Practical Tip: When uploading a presentation to SlideShare, make sure the first page of the presentation describes your topic visually and compels viewers. Do not use first pages of corporate templates. Add your contact information to the last slide and describe your competence to encourage people to get in touch with you.

This overview presents only the tip of the iceberg of available social channels. Which channels should you use for your business? This question is, in many cases, the wrong one to start with. Look at channels from a broader perspective. Think of your business goals and how social networking can help. Envision the dialogs, campaigns and interactions possible in support of your goal. Where can you find your target audience and what can you do to win its members? How can you activate them? Only when you have answered these broader questions can you select your channels based on how the audience is likely to use them. Finding the services that matter and setting up the channels to start engaging is an important aspect of engaging in social. It is not the channel but the social interactions that will enable you to reach your goal.

Once you engage on the selected channel, make sure that you define the personality, interactions, functions and services that are delivered through this channel. Next, brand them based on your company or personal brand, to ensure that people have the user experience you envision. What it looks like, which information you provide, how you post, how fast you respond, how direct and convincing you are – all these things matter in developing and engaging in the channel.

The business impact of engaging in social media channels is improved efficiency and better reach in places where your audience is, allowing you to engage and activate your audience.

4.4. Content – sharing things that matter

The concept: Creating and seeding content that is relevant and appealing to your audience and making it easy to like, share and comment on.

The business impact: A quick way to plant your messages and have them recommended by your advocates to their respective audiences.

In media, content is king. In social media, the same is true. It is the content that provokes dialog and spreads throughout the social network. So, if you have good "social content" and if you make it easy to experience and interact with this content, people are likely to share it with a broad audience that will discuss and potentially even enhance it through their conversations.

4.4.1. Visual Stories

Historically, stories have been the essence of human experience. Stories give us context, and context helps us understand things. Stories inspire and motivate people to action.

Among other places, we can learn good storytelling from film making: how great characters are created, how their profound conflicts are defined and how to put plots into actions are only some of the things great film makers have perfected.

People enjoy storytelling and are excited by good stories. They like to comment on and share them with their friends in the social network. The story of the Hudson River emergency flight landing was spread millions of times.

Figure 4.13: Hudson River emergency landing on Twitter
Example of the dialog about the emergency plane landing on the Hudson River: people shared their emotions and insights and added additional links to the story.

Stories can also be told in a visual format. Pictures, videos, infographics and presentations are ways to tell stories visually. The reason for this is simple. Social media provides an endless stream of information and people scanning social media streams can easily identify the value of a visual element and are attracted to it. Emotions are conveyed easily in a visual story, making it simple, fun and informative to read and interesting to share.

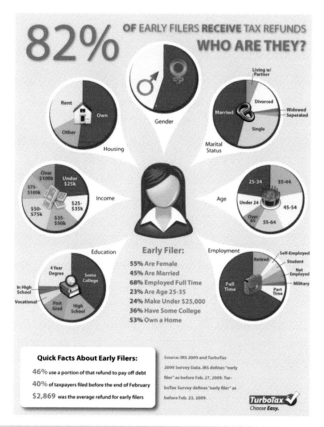

Figure 4.14: Example of an infographic, a popular social media format

This is an Infograph by TurboTax that visually depicts information about early tax filers.

Practical Tip: On Facebook, users can create albums of three or more pictures. When a user posts the album, Facebook will show the first three pictures next to each other, allowing you to tell a visual story. These stories have the highest interaction rates on Facebook.

4.4.2. Developing Content

But where does all this content come from? How do you develop it? Businesses often create a lot of content for their products and services. Reports, white papers, presentations, testimonials and video tutorials are useful and can be converted into a form that is easy to share and comment on. In addition, new content is constantly being generated for events, presentations, press interviews, trainings and other occasions. Agencies and partners are additional sources of content.

The social network is also full of good content, to which you can refer, comment on and re-share with your audience. In fact, it turns out that in most cases, creating good content is not the problem. It just needs to be adapted to social media. For that, it must be localized and optimized for social media viewing and spreading. It makes sense to plan ahead and develop a content plan to help achieve your goals. Experience shows that 50% of the content should be planned and 50% of the content should be developed on the spot, related to what is happening right now. This ensures relevance to current topics of interest and engagement. When and how you position the content of your dialog is essential to its success, so it must be aligned with your audience. Remember: content is king: make it distinguished and extraordinary.

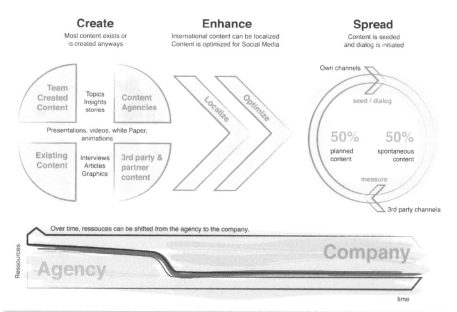

Figure 4.15: Creating social content
Content often exists in organizations or is created anyways for other media. Sources include the internal team, existing content, content agencies or third parties, such as partners. This content can be localized and optimized for social media. It can then be spread by engaging in dialog.

The business impact of sharing good content is that it can easily be commented on and shared and can be carried by your audience through the network.

Practical Tip: It is simple to optimize presentations for social media. They are easy to consume and share and provide a great way to show your knowledge. Make sure they get to the point fast and add real value to the person viewing them. Add a call to action and some questions to encourage dialog.

4.5. Monitoring and Measuring – listen to and learn from people

The concept: Listen to and understand what people say and do in the global social network to better understand their wishes and needs and profit from their insights. Monitor all your activities and measure success.

The business impact: Gain insights to make better decisions based on what your target audience really thinks and does. Avoid costly product, marketing and service mistakes.

4.5.1. Monitoring

Imagine you are in a room with Mark Zuckerberg (Facebook, CEO), Ashton Kutcher (actor), Lance Armstrong (cyclist) and Barack Obama (U.S. president). That is what social networking virtually allows you to experience. In addition to your neighbors, family members, friends, customers and colleagues, you will also find important people from all parts of society in the social network. In fact, we believe everybody who has a smart phone will be on social media in some form or other in the long run, because it enables people to connect and communicate. People will not want to be left out.

Social media gives you the ability to listen to what people say and do, see how they interact and understand their opinions and values. It gives you a window into people's behavior, thinking and attitudes. You can listen to public conversations and interactions on a global scale. You can tap into any conversation happening right now, as well as conversations that happened in the past. You'll be surprised at what you can discover and learn.

"Social media monitoring" tools provide you with unprecedented capabilities. They store and index all the conversations and posts that have occurred on any social media platform and analyze them for you. What people are saying about your brand, what people think about your products and services, what the competition says and does, what the fastest-growing audiences are for your market, which communication channels work best at what time and how effective your communication is: this is just a partial list of what can be analyzed and answered with social media monitoring. Using the best tools and applying intelligence in filtering and working with the data generates valuable reports, from which key insights can be extracted. These can help you understand what is happening in the mind of the consumer, and gain insights into key areas of your business. This is a marketing professional's dream since the first step to marketing is to understand your market and your customers.

You can use professional tools or you can engage professional services. At this point we recommend professional services, as the data can easily be skewed if the tools are not set up and the data not filtered properly. Professionals can filter out repeated or irrelevant messages and read and interpret the data properly.

One of the key advantages of social media monitoring vs. traditional research is that it taps into balanced opinions. People who talk with their peers about a given topic have the opportunity to develop a balanced opinion. People in the social network are not influenced by questionnaires from research companies or vendors as is common in traditional market research. Instead, they talk freely on any given topic.

Tapping into the social network and listening to what is being said, as well as extracting insights, allows you to better understand your market. It is an essential ingredient in making the right decisions on which markets to go after, which topics to address, which channels to choose, which campaigns to run and how to run them. It helps you understand your social resource and your potential in social media. Therefore, social media monitoring is an essential element of any successful social resource development and should be seen as a long-term and ongoing investment.

The business impact of monitoring is gaining a good understanding of your audience's needs and wants and providing a good basis for better decision making.

Practical Tip: Before engaging in social media, run a social media monitoring report to understand which channels people use to talk about your topics of interest, your company, your products and the competition. Understand the key trends and top issues, or those things that are missing from the conversation. This will allow you to be effective right from the start once you engage.

4.5.2. Measuring

Due to the digital nature of the social network, you can measure your activities and their impact on a broad scale. How many people respond to your dialog? How many people like your content? How many people visit your website based on the social interaction? These are some of the basic elements. However, these measurements provide no indication of whether you are successful in achieving your business goals. A more integrated approach is needed here.

To measure business impact, you must first define your company's key performance indicators (KPIs) for measuring your business. It is important to select KPIs that are really relevant. What keeps you up at night? Which indicator do you want to improve over the next 12 months? Once you've selected these, consider how you can achieve or support them using social media. Which social media indicators support your business KPIs and how can you measure them? This requires considerable effort but is very important for measuring and optimizing continuously. Some of the social media indicators such as share-of-voice, sentiment, active advocates, registrations, sales, etc. will have to be combined to provide your business KPI.

Practical Tip: When selecting social media KPIs, focus on what keeps you up at night. Select only one or two business indicators that are really important to you. Focusing on those will ensure that you are committed to putting resources into this effort and will provide you with the necessary drive and motivation to be successful. It will also ensure you are not spending time on generating things that are not directly relevant to your business, such as generating a lot of fans. It will also make it easier for you to take measurements.

Today's social media strategies often fall short on this. Measuring the downloads of a social app gives no indication of the value of the service to your customers. However, measuring what people do with the app helps you understand their needs, wants and likes. Analyzing all the data in social media is really rewarding and gives you the insights to take the right decisions and to be successful in leveraging your social resource in the long run.

Let us be clear: unless you measure extensively, it is unlikely you will be able to achieve the benefits.

Practical Tip: If you can't measure it, don't do it.

4.6. Advertising and search – searching and being found

The concept: Social dialog increasingly affects the ability to be found in search engines and social advertising enables new and effective advertising opportunities.

The business impact: More effective online marketing.

4.6.1 Advertising

Let's look at the social advertising revolution: The problem with traditional advertising is that it is difficult to target and results in a lot of wastage and inefficiency. People are overwhelmed, feel disturbed and therefore become resistant or immune to advertising. Now imagine advertising with little wastage, providing instant value. Because people share and engage in a dialog, the social network is full of valuable and real-time profile information. Imagine you, as an advertiser, can select the exact profile of your audience, based on profile and interactions: where they live, how old they are, how many kids they have, how often they go on vacation, what brands they like, what events they visit, what they are doing and thinking right now.

This is possible in social advertising, a new and evolving field of marketing. On Facebook, for example, you can select detailed profiles and provide ads based on the fan pages people like. For example, if you live in San Francisco, and like Jamie Oliver, BMW, Bulgari and great resorts on Facebook, you might be open to a weekend hotel special in at a 5-star hotel in Nappa Valley. On average, people check their Facebook streams five times each day. With hundreds of millions people doing so, the reach of your targeted ads can be huge. In addition, if you have the right offer, one that is interesting to the target group you select and relevant at the right moment, the click-rates can be impressive. Not only can you link to a website from the ad, you can also get a "like" for your Facebook page. This opens up a long-term communication channel between you and the user, allowing you to communicate with him over time, potentially every day. That is a significant result from a simple ad. Potentially, the person may not only become your customer, he may also become your advocate and actively help you achieve your business goals by influencing other potential customers from his circle.

Figure 4.16: Social advertising based on the profile of a user interested in social media
Example of an advertisement based on the profile of a user interested in social media marketing, analytics and CRM.

Practical tip: When defining your ad, start by envisioning your best customer profile and describe him in social terms like demographics, location, brand and services he might like. Then target only that profile. Measure your results and then expand to broader audiences. This will help you be effective with your resources and to ensure you only get the right audiences.

New advertising formats are constantly evolving to advertise within the context of social relations. If one of your social media friends has liked or commented on a brand, the brand can use that as an effective ad format for activating new users in this friend's network. On Facebook, these ads are called sponsored stories and are quite effective because they are trusted. Socially networked users are very interested in seeing what their trusted friends buy and recommend.

Figure 4.17: Sponsored stories
Dialog with friends are converted to ad by marketers.

4.6.2. Search

The next step in the evolution of the social network will be "social search." Today, you can search the Internet, including popular social media sites, using search engines. On the results page, you can see suggestions by advertisers and search engine results, which are based on an algorithm of relevance (based on content, links and frequency, among other things). These are highly influenced and optimized by the website owners. Companies spend millions on this, since it is so beneficial to be findable when people are looking for your product or service.

Social media changes this and the search engine companies are embracing the changes based on their own interests. Technically speaking, most social media dialogs have their own URLs, enabling them to be referenced and/or liked. Each dialog is counted as a link to you and has a positive effect on your search-engine ranking. Moreover, these dialogs can be found through search engines. This means people can find your dialogs about how satisfied people are with a product, how they plan to use it, why they will buy it again, etc. This is powerful in building opinions. Popular search engines like Google are now embracing this and are even displaying the profile picture of the people that recommended something in the search results. This has a very positive effect on the people who are searching. If a person sees 10 search results seeking a hotel in Rome, the one entry that has the profile picture of their friend on it is the one the person is likely to look at first. Has that person stayed there? Does he recommend it? People can even connect with other people in real time to talk to them and their search can stop there.

Getting Firefox To Save With Page Title As Filename 🔍
23 Feb 2005 ... See Extension For Getting **Firefox** To Save Pages Using Page Titles. ...
theiphonedoc on iPhone 4 Case Options (Try Some Old Cases! ...
daggle.com/getting-**firefox**-to-save-with-page-title-as-filename-6 - Cached - Similar
📷 Danny Sullivan shared this

persistent.info: Gmail Conversation Preview Bubbles 🔍
21 Aug 2005 ... I cannot install GM 0.6.4 on **Firefox** 1.5.0.1 b/c it says "not compatible". This
is very strange b/c I could get them all work on another Mac ...
blog.persistent.info/.../gmail-conversation-preview-bubbles.html - Cached - Similar
📷 Mihai Parparita shared this

Figure 4.18: Social advertising results in Google
An example of a social search result in Google, when looking for a social media consultant. You can see who shared this consultancy and ask that person to review their experience.

4.6.3. Google+ and social search

Google leverages its strength in social search. The Google+ network with the +1 button integrates tightly with the search engine. Clicking the +1 button results in better ranking of the content. Google adds a profile picture of the person who +1ed the content if they are connected to you. This allows you to see who liked and recommended the content directly in the search results. This provides trusted information and facilitates a direct communication channel with the person recommending the article.

Practical Tip: Add the Google +1 button to all your content and encourage people to click it. This will increase your relevance in search and will ensure you are ranked higher in the search results page. This also enables social search on Google, making the results more relevant to your audience.

In developing your social resource, your social search strategy is an essential building block. Leveraging social advertising and encouraging dialogs to increase social search effectiveness are only some of the ways of benefitting from this new development. We believe the relevance of content generated by people you know and trust will change search forever.

4.7. Social apps – services that multiply

The concept: Provide focused apps with built-in social interaction, information and service to activate new audiences.

The business impact: Increase your engagement with your audience and get them to recommend you as well as to help discover and engage new customers.

16 billion apps have been downloaded on the Apples iOS platform alone (source: en.wikipedia.org/wiki/App_Store_(iOS)). People love and frequently use apps, because they are little helpers designed to be very good at doing one focused thing. They are also easy to use, intelligent and often aesthetically pleasing and entertaining. It takes seconds to download and install these little helpers and for most people they have become part of everyday life.

Now that these apps are going social, let's look at an example of a "social app" and the benefits it offers.

Running enthusiasts spend hours training each week. Being entertained and seeing their training statistics are important elements of their motivation. Using the Nike+ app both entertains runners and offers them tracking features. It is also easy to use, with a beautiful interface. A few years ago, Nike added Facebook integration. This allowed runners to post their runs on Facebook and Twitter and gave the runner's friends the ability to comment on their friends' runs (e.g., "Great, let's run together," "how do you motivate yourself to run at 6 am?," "were you carrying a backpack, because you are so slow.") Nike+ reads the Facebook comments to you in real time as you run. In addition, Nike offers a running community, so a runner can run against friends and other runners in the virtual space, check his training progress and motivate himself and other runners.

Lindsay Brust

I just started a run with Nike+ GPS
Trying to go 30 min.

Cheer me on with comments or likes and I'll hear it along the way.

↩ 51 minutes ago via Nike Application · 🔒 · Like · Comment

👍 **Jason Cormier** and **Patti Sutula** like this.

| Write a comment... |

Figure 4.19: Nike+ Social App, sharing the runs on Facebook
This social app is extremely useful for Nike. It allows the company to see when people run, where they run and how often they run. Nike can motivate runners to run every day. And runners share their runs frequently and help activate other people to run and to use the Nike+ system. Runners also find their social capital increasing significantly when they run and motivate others to do so, too. The business benefit for Nike is clear. Better customer relationships, decreased marketing costs and increase in sales for Nike+ products.

Another social business app example is Yammer, the social network for people inside companies. People can use their mobile phones to update the status of what they are doing, what they are working on, any problems they encounter. Other people in the organization, even in other countries, can follow the conversation, even when working from a customer's site to benefit from the dialog or add value. Searching for topics like customers, products, etc. facilitates the generation of valuable insights.

There is a huge potential as apps go social. We expect more and more devices to go social as well. Navigation systems, TVs, and cars, for example, are all going social, adding value by adding and integrating social communication and services.

The business impact of social apps is in providing a built-in recommendation engine that is activated by users of the product.

Practical tip: Think about how to enhance your products and services by adding digital apps and making them social. This will allow you to offer new value, differentiate from your competition and add stickiness.

4.8. Social CRM – always be with your customer

The concept: The social network allows you to have a direct and persistent connection and communication channel with your customers. You can use that channel to strengthen the relationship and offer valuable services.

The business impact: Efficiency in marketing and service operations, more insights into what moves your customers.

Becoming networked with your customers provides you with a link and an opportunity for constant communication. This, in turn, allows you to develop a long-term relationship, which can be valuable to both sides. Using a simple dialog, you inform your customers of what you are doing and how they can benefit from new products. They can also communicate directly by asking questions, making suggestions, pointing out relevant information, events and activities, as well as comment on current topics of relevance. Based on this relationship, you encourage your customers to respond, interact and spread your messages. This dialog is an optimal form of customer relationship management (CRM), enabling dialog and constant interaction. It can be tracked and traced and can help you to achieve better CRM. For it to be valuable, your communication should be based on your vision, which your customers, ideally, share.

Working with your social resource also allows you to provide better and more efficient customer service. You can answer customer's questions and other people can see the answers and, if they wish, contribute, creating an efficient service community. Customers trust open service communication because they feel that companies are more genuine in this space than when answering a phone call.

Customer feedback and engagement can also be used in product and service development. It turns out that customers are happy to answer questions, give their insights and talk about their needs, if they see a value in the relationship with you. And you as a company can learn from the dialog with your customers what they really need and want.

Analyzing your social customer relationships allows you to generate important insights into their needs and their behavior, as well as important insights and trends that companies can use to provide better products and services as well as gain marketing and customer support efficiency.

Practical tip: Contact your CRM supplier to understand their social CRM offerings. Most CRM companies have picked up on this topic and provide out-of-the-box solutions or add-ons. Before implementing, be sure to define the KPIs needed to measure the impact and ensure that your CRM solution is capable of providing these KPIs.

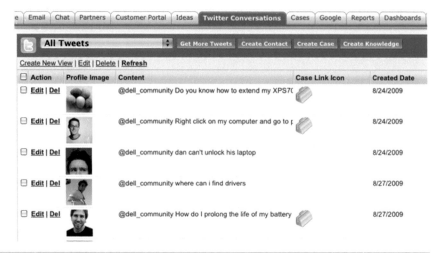

Figure 4.20: Social CRM screenshot from Salesforce, monitoring and interacting with customers through Twitter
Using social CRM, companies using the Salesforce CRM System can monitor the dialog of their customers on Twitter and identify issues or opportunities. They can directly engage, and create cases or insights based on a customer's conversations.

4.9. Commerce – using the social currency

The concept: Initiating transactions based on social interactions and using social capital as currency to activate users.

The business impact: Drive sales based on recommendations and impulse purchases and gain efficiency in marketing and winning sales.

People often discuss products and services and their experiences with them in social media, initiating dialogs and discussions with their friends. As a result, products are described, evaluated and recommended by the social network. This creates mindshare for these products and opinions, which if favorable, can be converted into a trusted sale.

There are multiple ways of doing this. Posting a beautiful video nudges people to ask which camera was used to create it, listening to a song and posting it gets people to evaluate the artist, checking into a restaurant motivates people to try it out themselves. If you want to benefit from an impulse purchase, you have to be present right at the moment when people are discussing the product. You can engage in the conversation and make a recommendation or an offer. Keep in mind that it must provide value to the user.

Smart companies motivate people to share their positive experiences in their social networks, and make offers and location specials to activate their users. There are many options available today, but we believe we are at the beginning of social commerce. Due to its direct impact on the bottom line, a lot of energy and creativity will flow into this field. Checking in to a place to get a special deal, getting additional services when liking a product, seeing in-stream offers in places where products are discussed, group buying to reduce the price and promoting this in people's social streams are only a few ways to get commerce into the social game.

You should not underestimate the efficiency of people recommending your product. How much marketing do you have to invest to get your product recommended in traditional channels? In the social network, there are efficient ways and incentives for doing this. Concepts such as pay-with-a-Tweet allow people to get a financial benefit for recommending a product. The restaurant Dom-Spatzen in Cologne, Germany gives users a free beer if they post that they are enjoying their time at the restaurant. Doing so spreads this positive message to all of the user's fans, perhaps inspiring them to visit the restaurant also. Using people's social networks and reach to drive sales is powerful and effective. The reach, combined with social capital, can be used as social currency. It can be traded into real value, products and money. Working with social resources allows you to tap into this game and drive product and service sales for your organization.

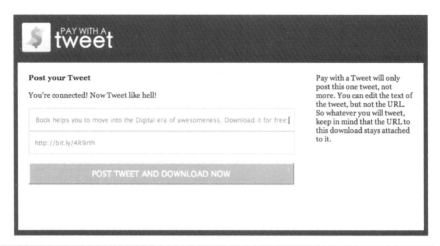

Figure 4.21: Pay with a Tweet
Pay with a Tweet is a concept that encourages people to Tweet about a product and then get a service or reward for doing so. The reward for spreading a positive message and recommendation can be a digital resource like a book or a song from an album, or a free beer at a restaurant.

These aspects are important drivers of social commerce. But be aware that this incentive only works for very good products and services. This is because people only recommend good products and experiences. They are just as fast in criticizing products, if they don't fit their needs or expectations.

Practical Tip: Only select very good products and services for social commerce and ensure the overall experience is optimal. This will improve the chances that people will like and recommend your products. It will also help you avoid having more negative than positive experiences shared through the social network.

4.10. Campaigns – activate your users

The concept: Initiate and drive ideas through the social network that move and activate people in your favor based on your idea.

The business impact: Gain reach and activate people on your behalf.

Campaigns unite all the previously described social elements and combine their forces in activating people to reach a certain business goal. Social campaigns define a goal that is relevant to the aligned people, provide a means to reach this goal as well as an infrastructure for running the campaign and activate the social resources to work together to reach this goal.

Barack Obama ran a well-planned social-media campaign to win the U.S. presidential election against all odds to become the first African-American president. He tweeted daily about his engagements and thoughts on how to change the nation for the better; he gave people digital tools to spread his message and to support fundraising, making it the most successful campaign ever, both financially and in terms of the sheer number of people involved and the results achieved.

Figure: 4.22: Campaign by Barack Obama to activate people (i.e., ask a friend to join)
Mobile website of the Barack Obama campaign, asking members to spread the Barack Obama campaign among their friends.

For efficient campaigning, the following questions should be considered before defining details:

- Why are you engaged in the campaign and why should people care?
- How are you developing your campaign, so it will become special and people will join you and activate their social resources?
- What are you doing to run the campaign and activate the users?

Based on the answers you come up with, the campaign should consist of the following elements:

- Set up necessary building blocks – channels, dialog plan, content, apps, advertising, search, etc. These need to be integrated for the user into a coherent campaign concept.
- Create a good user experience throughout the communication process – making it easy for users to understand what to do and why to do it.
- Provide strong motivation for people to participate and share – you should know why your audience cares.
- Offer optimal interaction among the various elements of the campaign – it should be easy for your audience to participate and benefit from the campaign.
- Define the scope of initial reach for the campaign at start – you should have a plan for how to make people aware of the campaign before it starts spreading in the social network.
- Come up with a content and dialog plan – you should plan 50% of your content and dialog, the rest you can develop as the campaign is executed. This will ensure you are always prepared.
- Plan for contingencies – have emergency measures in place in case something goes wrong and dialog gets out of hand.
- Determine how results are measured and communicated – create an integrated measuring process and a score card for the results.
- Brainstorm about what else can be done to support the campaign in other channels – think about your other channels, how can they support the campaign, and vice versa.

When selecting the team for your social campaign, you should ensure that you have at least one person who is experienced in social media campaigning. The learning curve can be quite steep, and you will learn faster and avoid making too many mistakes if you have an experienced person on your team.

At that point, you are ready to launch your campaign. You should monitor and optimize continuously, until the campaign achieves the desired results.

In the social network, outcomes and dynamics are hard to predict and interactions can be quite complex. Therefore, we recommend that you use an agile process for managing the campaign. You should be able to incorporate the constant learning and to react quickly to changing situations and developments. We have developed a social scrum approach, inspired by the scrum programming method in modern software development. While the overall goal is clear, the campaign is divided into chunks of small goals to be reached. The team works to achieve these in a short span of time. The campaign work can be exposed in the social network, where people appreciate the work and can integrate themselves with their ideas and support to make the campaign successful.

Practical Tip: When creating campaigns, use the WOW! method. Ask yourself why are you are engaged in this campaign, why should people care? Then define how the campaign is special and how it works. Finally, define what you are going to do. "What?" should always be the last question, never the first.

Summary

- Leveraging the social media resource for your business requires you to grow your social network by engaging in valuable dialog and providing good content and value-added services to your audience.
- In this chapter we offer many tools, tips and tricks to support your efforts.
- Be aware that being successful with your social resources requires time and effort and cannot be achieved overnight. Just like your brand, your social resource has to be built over time.
- In developing, you should be authentic and focus on your strengths.
- Always focus on the WOW! method.
- Measuring and monitoring are important to understanding your audience and optimizing your activities in order to reach your goals successfully.

5. How to Use your Social Resource to Create Measurable Business Impact

In order to achieve significant business value, you have to select an area that is crucial for your company. You should have the competence and it should be a fit with your corporate culture. In this chapter we show how the company innovation process, the customer service process and conquering new markets provide significant opportunities for leveraging the social resource in your favor. Understanding why and how to do it is important to achieving your goals when actually doing it.

In many aspects, the social resource can provide enormous power and energy for companies. If aligned and activated, it can have a significant impact on your company's competitiveness and bottom line. We expect the social resource to have a groundbreaking impact on the way we conduct business in the future. In fact, it is likely to change the way companies work and think, and has the potential to change the boundaries of our economies.

Today, many companies work isolated within closed office buildings. Various units and departments focus on developing strategies to differentiate and conduct their business efficiently. Often, they operate in silos. Employees enter company buildings each morning to work with their colleagues in creating value for the company. They spend their time in internal meetings and discussions, communicating mostly sequentially, with limited communication among units, departments, countries. Customer communication is mainly a monolog.

This way of operating does not allow companies to build social capital, nor does it enable companies to develop their social resources and put them into action for achieving their business goals. To change this, companies must rethink the way social dialog is conducted. We believe quick communication with colleagues to exchange ideas and learning across an enterprise, direct dialog with partners and customers, listening to market needs and movements will be the new standard for winning in the socially networked enterprise area. Companies will engage in an agile living network driven by the social resource.

All efforts and communication will center around the corporate vision and mission, with the goal of increasing the value of the corporation. Competitiveness, sustainability, operational excellence, brand building, marketing effectiveness, sales performance and product innovation will be just some of the areas likely to benefit.

In this section, we focus on putting the social resource into action for real business benefit. For this, we will look at three concrete business scenarios.

5.1. The company innovation process

Companies must innovate to stay ahead of the market and to survive. In good organizations, this innovation happens at all levels: products, processes, communication, collaboration, administration, etc. A company's ability to generate these innovations and put them into action is often a decisive factor in the company's prosperity and future potential. Companies take great care to establish their innovation processes and culture within their organization. They allow innovation to be planned, resourced and well-managed by dedicated groups. Increasingly, the innovation process has evolved into collecting and filtering diverse ideas, developing them, acceptance-testing them and deploying them in products and processes.

Today, it is possible to tap into a much larger pool of individuals both internal and external to the business for innovative ideas. The social resource of any company can bring tremendous innovation, with fresh ideas and concepts for products, processes, communication, collaboration and management. Your customers, consultants, partners and employees are often those with the best insights into your products and processes. They form the best social resource for suggesting innovative ideas that may result in breakthroughs. Because of the importance of this process and the direct business impact, especially in product and service innovation, this process can take years to yield benefits and requires huge capital and human resources. Will it deliver the best ideas? Will the innovations really be adopted by the market? How difficult will it be to market them? Will the business case work? The success of your company is at stake!

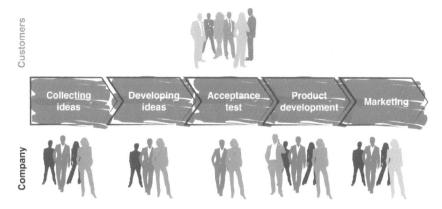

Figure 5.1: Today's innovation process takes years
The innovation process is often divided into stages. Companies have tight control over the process and have dedicated teams for each stage. Customers are involved only during the acceptance phase.

Now let's put the social resource into action. At first, we focus on the fundamental success factor: generating the right ideas. How can you ensure your innovation team comes up with the right idea? Can you rely on a few good minds to scan the broad range of possibilities and discover the best potential? It's time to open up your innovation process.

Challenge your social resource to engage in the innovation process. Make it part of your quest to find and deliver the best possible innovation, one that is aligned with your company's vision. Make the members of your social resource understand that they are doing this for themselves and their own networks. Let them know how they will benefit from engaging by enjoying the best product innovation based on their input and guidance. Make them part of your team and lead them to success.

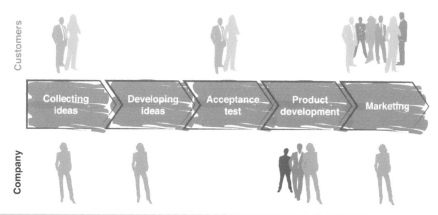

Figure 5.2: Company innovation process with the social resource can take months instead of years
Using social media, companies can engage with their social resource in collecting ideas, then acceptance test and market a product to limit some of the cost of product development and gain products with better customer acceptance.

Aligning your social resource with your vision for this quest is essential. Communicate and interact with this group directly, explain what you are going to and how you plan to do it. Communicate your intentions and your program in great detail, as you would do with your internal innovation team and be open to their feedback and suggestions. This can easily be done through a social website. Use this to recruit those resources that have a lot of social capital and are best aligned. Only if they are aligned can they find the best ideas based on their needs, use all of their creativity and find a solution that is right for you. Give them tools to activate their own social resources in the process. Build a social media app (such as a Facebook app) to make it easy for them to contribute, discuss and share with you and their socially networked friends. Allow them to understand the entire process, how ideas will be decided upon, put into action and to market.

You will be surprised how quickly they will generate relevant ideas you may never have thought of. Because the members of your social resource are likely to be potential consumers of your products, they know and understand their needs and how they can be best met. Make the ideas transparent to inspire everyone to think even further, vote, discuss and verify the potential with your social resources. Make the idea selection process transparent and open. Be sure that you lead the process. You are the one that has to invest the company's resources to make the idea work. You have to be the guide in ensuring the ideas are achievable as well as perfectly aligned with your business goals, your competence and your corporate culture.

Once you have selected an idea, pick the contributors from your internal and external social resources and collaborate with them to develop a detailed concept. Take an agile project management approach to be quick to identify the main areas of innovation and the cornerstones of its success. Use rapid prototyping to get a sense of the total innovation experience. You might want to look at your competition and other innovations happening in parallel.

At this stage, you invite your engaged social resources for the acceptance test. Allow people to comment on and share to learn quickly and to understand the market dynamics. Of course this cannot be done in all cases and might require a non disclosure agreement. Taking a more open approach, however, is useful in understanding additional implications for marketing, sales and service and brings more horsepower to your innovation process.

Now develop your product and bring all your competence, resources and direction to that process. Early product versions can be shown, shared and discussed with your social resources, enabling you to get continuous feedback and make important adjustments. This helps to ensure the product is on track and also meets the demands and serves the needs of potential customers.

Once the product is completed, you can work with your social resource to bring the product to market. Reward your social resources for engaging in the process. Give them and their friends early access to the product, allow them to communicate their engagement and spread the message. You will likely be rewarded by the enthusiasm and engagement they spread among their social resources. Make them your heroes. This is likely to inspire others to help you in the future as well as increase your social capital, since people can experience how you work with your social resources and customers.

If done right, you can shorten your innovation process from years to several months and you can achieve many more tangible business benefits.

Of course, you will need to manage the innovation process carefully. Select which information to give and ensure that your intellectual property is protected as you open up your innovation process. Not all phases can be opened in the process if you need to protect intellectual property. Also consult the current best practices on the web, which can easily be identified using search.

Let's look at some of the business indicators that show the competitiveness and business mechanics of your social innovation process.

<u>You achieve an increase in customer acceptance through:</u>

Valid discovery of existing and relevant customer needs by lead users

    →   Increase the satisfaction of customer needs

Increase in number and diversity of ideas through integration of users ideas

    →   Increase number of ideas

<u>Decrease your cost of innovation by:</u>

Shifting some of the task in the innovation process to your social resource (crowd sourcing)

→	Decrease research and development costs

Reducing the cost of innovation through multiplication effects and viral spreading (earned media)

→	Decrease market entry costs

Gaining higher customer acceptance, reducing development costs and avoiding costs associated with product market failures (flops)

→	Increase innovation success quota

Reduce the time to market through:

Utilizing externally developed concepts and prototypes (crowd sourcing)

→	Decrease time to concept

More processes run in parallel; communication and collaboration are more efficient

→	Decrease time to develop

Minimizing time for acceptance tests

→	Decrease time to launch

You can achieve three key performance indicators that prove the effectiveness of the social innovation process:

- Increase customer acceptance
- Decrease cost of overall innovation efforts
- Decrease time to market

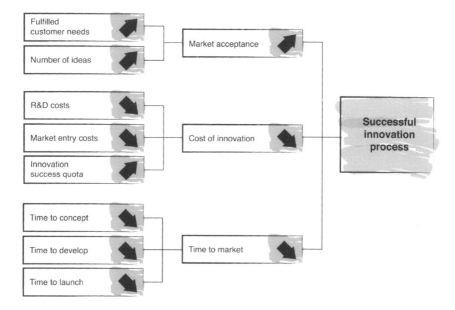

Figure 5.3: Benefits of leveraging the social resource in the innovation process
The innovation process becomes more successful by increasing the market acceptance of the resulting products, reducing both the cost of innovation and the time to market.

To understand the mechanics of the innovation process, let's look at a concrete example:

5.2. My Starbucks Idea

People like Starbucks for its great products, the good feeling associated with them and the atmosphere in the stores. Their experiences are often discussed in their social networks. Can Starbucks continue to evolve as a leading coffee company? Do the 137,000 employees have the best ideas for the best products of the future? As early as 2008, Starbucks created the concept of My Starbucks Idea. This allowed people to submit ideas in the categories of product, experience and involvement as well as describe what they would suggest or like to see in Starbucks stores. All the ideas submitted could be seen in public and people could vote on which idea they found useful and would like to see. After the transparent selection process, Starbucks made transparent the way in which the idea is put into action and thus let the user participate in the process. Even Starbucks employees use the site to submit their innovations.

Figure 5.4: My Starbucks Idea
By engaging the social resource, customer needs are better fulfilled, the number of ideas increases, the cost of innovation goes down, while the time to concept as well as the time to market decreases. This gives significant business benefits to Starbucks.

The results are stunning. Starbucks achieved significant profits from the new products and improved the overall customer experience.

More than 70,000 product ideas, more than 300 put into action.

More than 30,000 experience ideas, more than 150 put into action.

More than 15,000 involvement ideas, more than 150 put into action.

(source: mystarbucksidea.force.com)

This can only work if you have built your social resource and can activate it for your mission. If you have enough social capital and alignment, you can achieve your business goals.

5.3. The customer service process

Customer service is often the place where the customer gets direct exposure to the company. The quality of customer service has a huge impact on your brand and customer loyalty. This is why companies spend a lot of money optimizing this experience. Great customer service creates repeat buyers and positive recommendations. Customers today value service that is fast, personal, hassle-free, easy to access and easy to use. Customer service is really a social part of the organization, the component that is all about how people help people with a problem. Social media is all about people interacting with people. A business can use many different resources in providing good customer service. The social resource of any company can be leveraged to provide better customer service. Your customers are often the best social resources for helping other customers by using social media. Customers who have resolved a service issue can be aligned, activated and incentivized to help other customers in a similar situation. Saving costs in customer service, while increasing customer satisfaction and loyalty, is the holy grail of customer service. Let us put the social resource into action to show how you can achieve this.

Take, for example, this concrete scenario. A customer has a problem with his new mobile phone. For some reason, he cannot connect his laptop to the phone to access the Internet on his computer through the phone. He waits for the opening hour of his supplier's customer service hotline to connect with a customer service agent, who readily supports the customer. Because of the complexity of the issue, the need to troubleshoot both the phone and the laptop, the customer service representative has to engage a product technician to help solve the problem. Thirty minutes later, the problem is fixed. The time of the support agent and the technician, their training and availability costs are enormous. Moreover, other people had to wait in the call line, complaining to the company's management. How can this be done better?

First, we can broaden the accessibility of the customer services by adding social media channels as an opportunity for customers to consult the customer service. This is useful since it is asynchronous. A question posed in the evening can be answered by the support representatives in the morning hours, an arrangement that is readily accepted if communicated clearly on the company's website. In addition, other people can see the question and might offer a quick solution. They can consult the customer and share their experiences with the product. Other people can follow the dialog and solve their problems based on the information given. In this way, the power of the social resource, with all its knowledge and experience, can be put to work. Customer service can give additional tips and add value, giving a positive spin to the conversation as it spreads through the social network.

In addition, the social media customer service can be made searchable. Customers experiencing a problem can consult the service channel and search for a problem before actively posting or calling the hotline. Because of the reach of social search, the answers can even be found in popular search engines just by entering the problem description in Google, for example.

Advanced companies create specific social service communities, in which people can interact and search based on problems, feedback, sharing ideas and giving praise. Giving praise is important to the motivation of the service team. It also spreads through the user's network and supports a positive image of the company.

A company can also expand and offer proactive support. Because companies can listen directly to their consumers, they can identify issues based on dialogs about problems and consumer suggestions. The company can actively use social media monitoring solutions and social search to find users that have problems, offer support and learn from. The reward is often a big thank you dialog from the user (users do not expect proactive support), which spreads through the web, supporting the image of the company.

Even product managers can tap into the knowledge and dialogs created to understand the performance and issues with their product to support them in better product development and management.

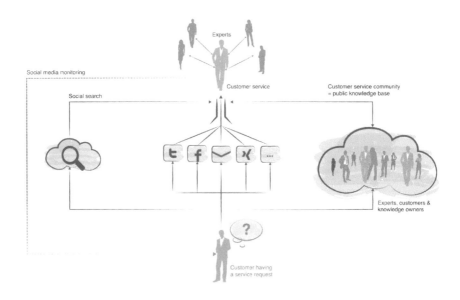

Figure 5.5: The social resource in the customer service process
Customers can communicate to companies through social media. This allows other people to follow the conversation and provide support. These conversations can be found in search to help people looking for solutions on the Internet, independent of their social media engagement. Customer service communities can be engaged to help customers proactively. Monitoring conversations generates important feedback to product experts.

The measurable benefits of doing all of this are huge. Let's map them to common customer service indicators:

The cost of the customer support organization decreases through the following indicators:

Active answering of service requests through other customers and knowledge bases

→   Number of delegated contacts (new indicator)

Active monitoring of social dialog about the company and its product and offering help and support

→   Number of found instances (new indicator)

Reduction of the number of cases and the solution time for each case by involving the social service community and knowledge database

→   Reduction of the cost per case

In addition, the availability of customer service personnel increases through the following indicators:

Opening of additional customer service channels that also work asynchronously in the relevant social sites

→   Increase in the number of communication channels

24/7 resolution of customer problems by the social service community and the knowledge base

→   Increase in service hours

An important factor for customer service success is the time it takes to solve each support issue. Let's see how this indicator decreases when the social resource is employed:

Reduction of the average time to react to a problem based on external support

→   Reduction of the time to react

Reduction of the average time to solve the problem based on external support

→   Reduction of the time to solve the issue

Better integration of customer service experts (2nd and 3rd level) as well as more competent solutions including public voting and ranking of the solutions

→   Increase in the number of solved problems

You can achieve three key performance indicators that prove the effectiveness of the social service community:

• Decrease in totals costs for customer service
• Increase in the availability and reachability of customer service
• Reduction of the time to solve problems

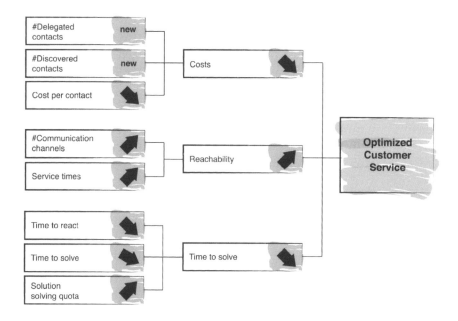

The following business example shows how the resource can be put into action in customer service.

5.4. AT&T Customer Care

Telecommunication products and service are very complex. Often the users are overwhelmed by the configuration options and struggle to get their equipment to operate as desired. AT&T is one of the biggest players in the market. The common understanding of people is that customer service is hard to reach, service representatives struggle to help and trying other service channels yields different answers.

This is why AT&T started a channel on Twitter. A Facebook channel followed some time later. These channels allow people to ask direct questions and engage in discussions with people who needed support or had ideas. Twitter users quickly spread the message and discussed the benefits of using this channel. The open dialogs and engagement of the customer service representatives were highly appreciated.

Figure 5.7: AT&T Customer Support Twitter channel
AT&T social media customer support benefits from a reduced cost per contact, the increase of communication channels, a decreased time to react and an increase in the number of solved issues.

Many AT&T customers are now using this as their primary service, when experiencing problems and looking for answers. In addition to answering questions, the company is using this to collect praise, suggestions and also promote special offers to its AT&T customer support users.

The social resource is highly engaged, offering its knowledge and support and helping to spread a positive image throughout social media.

5.5. Conquering new markets

A common way for companies to grow and improve their long-term profitability is to expand into new markets and grow their customer reach. To do this, they have to win new customers' hearts and minds. This is often a costly and long-term undertaking, since new customers are not likely to know or trust the new entrant. They are often lured by the competition that may be better known to potential new customers and may make them resistant to marketing efforts by a new company.

One of the biggest challenges to entering new markets is finding, identifying and winning the trust of potential new customers. Your social resource can help you discover, match-make and gain trust. The global reach of your social resource makes it an ideal bridge into the new market. Your customers, consultants, partners and employees generally have a wide network of latent business connections, making them the best social resource for bridging the gap to your new markets. Let's put the social resource to action!

A three-step approach has proven to be successful in conquering new markets: 1) win 2) align and 3) activate.

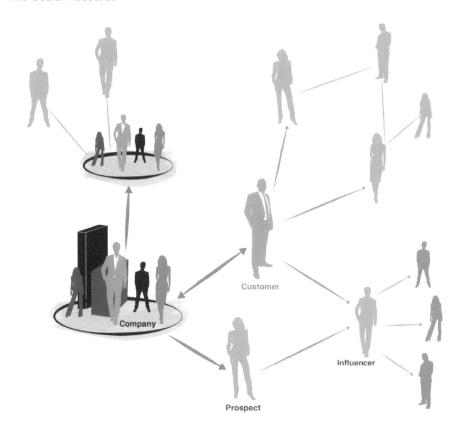

Figure 5.8: Leveraging social connections in conquering new markets
Brands can directly communicate with prospects and customers who, in return, spread their communication to their friends and connected influencers, allowing relevant dialogs to spread throughout the social network to reach new audiences.

Listening is essential to understanding your potential customers and to deciding which approach to take in entering the market. Using social media monitoring allows you to identify hot topics, measure volume of communication, and identify key influencers for given topics in order to understand the market dynamics. While there are many tools to cover specialized networks, we recommend engaging professional support in this early listening phase. Getting it right from the beginning ensures that you will move in the right direction and have the best possible chance to win. Based on monitoring, you can assess the market potential and define your market entry strategy. Calculating your social horsepower and that of your competition helps in assessing the business opportunity.

In the winning phase, you address your target audience to engage in dialog. It is important to be relevant and offer a vision, one that resonates with potential customers. Social advertising, search and social apps can help you target and engage relevant users. Since you are focused on your mission, be sure to provide valuable content related to your mission, be relevant to the user's needs and open in the communication of your goals. Be authentic and trustworthy! This can take some time, depending on the alignment of the audience with your vision. In some cases, it can develop faster than you would expect, based on the power of the social resource you engage.

Define a clear campaign for activating your users and work tightly with your social resources to win the market. Provide concrete engagements, calls to action, questions and answers and offers. Excite your users to join your mission. Highlight the benefits to them and be open to suggestions and critiques from your new market.

Taking the social approach to conquering new markets provides significant measurable business benefits. Let's look at some of the common business benefits:

Increase your reach through social media:

Gain broad reach for a socially active audience in social media

→   Increase in paid media with high efficiency

Benefit from free recommendations and spreading through your new and active social resource

→   Earned media (new indicator)

Increase your credibility with new audiences:

Trusted, positive environment, personal atmosphere

→   Positive environment increases

Intense interaction through social relationship, long-term dialog and engagement

→   Increase relationship power

Reduce the cost of market entry:

Reduce the average cost of reach by using the most efficient media

→   Cost per reach decreases

Ratio of paid-to-earned media increases

→   Cost for paid media is reduced

You can achieve three key performance indicators that prove the effectiveness of conquering new markets with your social resource:

- Increase your reach with social media
- Increase your credibility with new audiences
- Reduce the cost of market entry

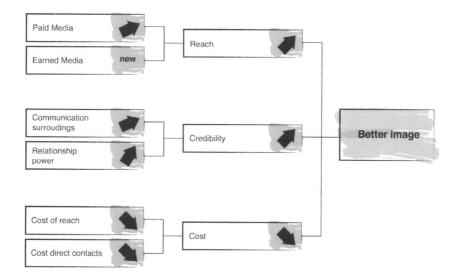

Figure 5.9: Benefits of the social resource in entering new markets
Companies can conquer new markets and improve their image through increased reach, increased credibility and decreased costs.

You should be aware that these benefits are only achievable if you have a good story and a product or service that targets an unmet need or is significantly better than your competitor's products. Understanding why people should care is very important.

Let us look at a concrete example to better understand the mechanics:

5.6. Introducing BMWi:

Personal mobility is on the verge of radical change. Oil as a natural resource is diminishing and cities are becoming more crowded. Mobility solutions will respond to this new environment. Electricity is a strong contender for replacing oil as the primary energy resource. "Born electric" is the motto of the new BMWi brand, focusing on totally new mobility solutions. Rethinking the mobility concept from the start, the company aims to win the heart of mobile people for a new, efficient, intelligent and social concept.

In entering the market, BMW taps into the social resource to help create, expand and market the concept in a fast and innovative way, with high user engagement.

Next to offering information and engagement in its social media channels, BMWi is partnering with the premier social media news site Mashable for concrete interactions and campaigns.

The global innovation series is one area in which Mashable and BMWi collaborate. The section "Drivers of change in the world of mobility" showcases the latest innovations in urban mobility. Articles and ideas are widely discussed and new ideas are submitted. Articles are discussed and shared, a real time Twitter feed shows what people are discussing at any given moment. The site shows users which of their friends are engaged and what they think and like about this revolution in mobility. The BMWi venture fund supports innovative start-up ideas around mobility to finance location-based mobile apps to enhance the mobility experience.

Within a few months of launching this offering, the BMWi brand spread and received engagement around the world. We believe this is just the start of a jointly developed mobile future independent of oil.

Figure 5:11: BMWi social website with Mashable (source: www.mashable.com)
BMW is partnering with Mashable, a popular social media site, to engage with users on the topic of electric mobility, asking users for their ideas on global innovation and allowing users to enter dialog, like and share the content.

Summary

- Always put your social resource into action in an area that really matters to you and that fits your competence and corporate culture. This will give you the focus and drive to be successful.
- The innovation process allows you to get valuable impulses and ideas from your customers, engages their know-how in the process, helps validate ideas, concepts and prototypes and provides a good story for marketing the products. Take care in managing the process to ensure you can deliver based on your core competence.
- Customer service is very rewarding for the overall brand experience and helps generate happier customers. Using the social resource helps you reduce costs and provide a better service experience.
- Conquering new markets can be efficient using the reach and targeting capabilities of social media. This only works if you have a good story and good products that meet people's unfilled needs or are significantly better that your competitor's products.

6. Social Enterprise Evolution

In this concluding chapter, we share our views on how the Internet and social media will continue to transform our society. Our focus is on how companies will look and operate when staffed by people who use their social resources naturally, every day, for most business functions. We start with the fundamental changes the Internet has brought about and established as the new normal. We then further develop ways in which the social resource can be used as a standard procedure by your employees and by all of your company's business partners.

The Internet and social media are rapidly reshaping the way we as a society communicate and deal with information. Since information and communication are the very fabric of our society, these information exchanges are transforming everything – our personal lives, our institutions, our businesses and our governments. We believe our society is only at the very beginning of this transformation, yet, it is already possible to develop a picture of where we are heading and how some changes will fundamentally and radically alter the way we will operate as a society. In this chapter, we look ahead to where social media may be taking us.

The Internet has fundamentally altered the role of information. Information is attached to everything we know – people, objects, locations, processes, finance, etc. The Internet has liberated information and given us free, instantaneous and global access to it, allowing us to make decisions and to act on the basis of this information. It has created five fundamental new capabilities that cut across all parts of our society:

- **Universal and instantaneous access** to information about everything from anywhere via the Internet and websites. This forms the foundation for the information revolution.
- **Search** of information across a universal information database and the organization thereof, based on relevance for immediate use, through popular search engines, foremost among them, Google. This has made access to the information useful to the masses.
- **Email** as a primary one-to-one and one-to-many communication method, with universal access and reach, laying the foundation for electronic communication. IP telephony chat, voice/video and conferencing add new dimensions to our communications portfolio, best exemplified by Skype.
- **Transactions** – commercial, business, process, and institutional – from anywhere, in any field. Online, we can shop for anything, book tickets, pay taxes, run factories, buy stock, bank, operate machines, from anywhere. This allows us to do things remotely, based on access to information over the Internet.
- **Targeting** based on the record of past activities and profile, as with Google ads. This increases the relevance of the Internet for businesses and individuals.

It took a few years for people, companies and institutions to absorb and then get used to these powerful capabilities, delivered through the Internet almost free of charge. Over time, the level of comfort has grown and the areas of application have exploded, making Internet use an indispensable and natural way of life for 2 billion people.

This pervasiveness is easily demonstrated when we lose our Internet connection, even for a short time, at home or work. In fact, most systems in developed and industrialized economies would now come to a standstill without the Internet. Developing countries are huge beneficiaries, with new efficiencies created by leapfrogging poor infrastructures of transport, information access and telecommunication.

The Internet revolution laid the foundation for the next phase of societal transformation: community-based communication through social networking. Internet access to information and transactions puts better tools in the hands of the masses to generate and publish information for others to consume, comment on and interact with. It has given them platforms on which to form self-defined communities of interest for sharing, exchanging and discussing. It has created a medium through which to express, contribute and share points of view and opinions in a variety of popular and industry-specific fora.

These have evolved over time into universal information sharing and discussion platforms such as Facebook, Twitter and Google+ as well as specialized sharing platforms such as Flickr, Picasa, YouTube and SlideShare. These are defining a new way of communicating and developing knowledge on almost everything as a group. It is a mass communication revolution. The key adjective for this phenomenon is "social." In this revolution, everything becomes social.

Social media is an outgrowth of the original Internet revolution. It has brought about the following five fundamental changes in our society, transforming the way in which we learn, decide and communicate:

- **Profiled people:** Every person has a self-created descriptive profile that is enhanced by activities, opinions, preferences, etc., over time, describing the person in increasing detail as a social entity. This information is selectively available to others to help them decide how to interact with this person. The profile is like a menu displayed outside a restaurant that helps a passerby decide whether he wants to eat there and what to order if he does.

- **Universal social tagging:** Every topic, location, event, person, etc. will become social. This means everything can be assigned attributes (tags) and descriptions (comments) by anyone and that all of these, collectively, become a virtual part of that object. Traditional media, e.g., newspapers and magazines, long dominated opinion shaping with their views. Social tagging makes it possible for everyone to express their views (tags) on everything (objects). This means everything is now "wrapped" in social opinions. Tools such as Foursquare make it easy to tag locations with your personal experience and viewpoint. Increasingly, our decision to select a restaurant, a book, a movie, a hotel or a vacation spot is determined by the social tags on that object, all of which can be accessed and evaluated in advance via social media. The prevalence of social tagging shows its tremendous potential impact.

- **Crowd sourcing** allows the combined insights and intelligence of the masses to be pooled for any opinion-forming and decision-making situation. Crowd sourcing fundamentally opens up access to the skills, insights, knowledge, experience and intelligence of your social resource. If used in the right way, this "free-of-charge consulting" can markedly enrich and streamline your decision making. It facilitates the integration of the hunches of many diverse people into innovative breakthroughs.

- **Open and transparent systems:** Everyone has the potential to contribute ideas, content and actions. This openness brings an amazing transparency to all systems. Nothing can be kept a secret. Someone is always able to discover the truth and publish it, either individually or collectively via discussions.
- **The social resource** is a new resource, derived from the social network. It is a self-selected, trusted, aligned and personalized subset of your overall social network. To reap its benefits, you need the skills and ability to nurture it, as we describe in this book.

An amazing number of tools and platforms keep coming to market to help you tap into your social resource so that all this becomes just as easy and natural for everyone as using the Internet. The driver of the social media revolution is the inherent need of people to communicate, share what they know, discover the views of other people on their areas of interest and the gratifying feeling that comes from helping others.

We believe we are at the outset of social media evolution. About half of the 2 billion people on the planet with Internet access have experienced social media through one of the most popular platforms, such as Facebook, Twitter or Google+. More than half of these – about 600 million – are regular social media users and their numbers are growing rapidly. We are still in the figuring-out stage of using social media technology. A lot of experimentation and innovation is taking place, which leads to a broad understanding, and, ultimately, expertise in the mass use of this new medium.

Now, let us project how our society might operate if 2 billion people were very well versed in the use of social media and used it with ease in all facets of their daily lives. Businesses would operate assuming all employees were as familiar with social media usage as they are with the PC, smart phones and the Internet. Let us assume, for the moment, that most privacy concerns of today have been addressed and resolved. Our outlook on the five social media mega changes encompasses:

- **Profile:** Everyone would have a publicly shared and fairly complete profile.
- **Social objects:** Everyone would actively tag their environments as naturally as they walk around and see the world. They would almost always use social tags to help make decisions on interactions with any objects or individuals.
- **Crowd sourcing:** Reliance on universal access to the opinions of people with skills, insights and knowledge from a diverse background would become the standard way of arriving at decisions about everything. Participating in crowd-sourcing exercises for others and sharing insights and expertise would become a standard daily activity.
- **Transparency:** Constant sharing of what you experience and observe and the insights you have would become second nature and simple, due to immense cloud-based systems that would organize this mass of information into manageable and useful categories. This would bring about total transparency on all issues.
- **Social resource:** Everyone would be adept at nurturing and leveraging their social resources in their personal, business and social lives. The social resource would be far larger and easier to manage as tools and platforms improve.

The social enterprise

In such a setting, how would a business be structured? How might it operate internally? Externally? With customers, partners, channels and social objects?

For a start, we believe most companies would be much more streamlined. They would have employees only for their core business functions and integration skills for the specific business. The company would be able to tap into the skills of its large social resource very efficiently, on a mutual basis, through a system of social incentives. It would be much easier to engage external consultants within the social resource on an ad hoc basis. With all employees socially open and socially skilled, leveraging the social resource would be considered a normal part of most jobs. Extensive use of tags on social objects would be used routinely in decision-making. Most problem solving would involve crowd sourcing within the social resource for high-quality, time-efficient results. Open culture would become a standard feature for companies. Openness would be across the board – within the employee base, with partners and extending to customers – one large community.

Summary

- The Internet is the biggest communication revolution of the last century, after telephones and radio. It has fundamentally changed the way in which we deal with information and communication.
- Social media has extended the revolution to group communication and has made everyone a publisher of original content. Information has been democratized, giving everyone a say.
- We believe that once we, mainstream global society, get familiar with and become natural users of social media – just as we have become users of computer and email – communication and information behavior will fundamentally change.
- Companies are likely to be far more streamlined and make much wider use of their social resources for most business processes.
- Competitiveness is likely to be driven by the efficient use of social resources.
- Since social resource usage is a mutual play – I help you and you help me – our society is likely to become much more interdependent.

Social X Glossary

Analytics: This is the science of analysis in the process of obtaining an optimal or realistic decision based on existing data. It is often used to gain a realistic insight into the efficiency of a program.

App: This is the new way of delivering an application. An app focuses on a specific user need and directly addresses it in a very easy-to-use fashion. Apple and Google have popularized apps as the fastest and most preferred way of delivering Internet-based services. They also have a much shorter development time.

Check-in: When a user tells Foursquare (a location-based mobile platform) where he is, this step is called "checking in." Users can check in from parks, bars, museums, restaurants, and libraries – really anywhere. When a user checks in, Foursquare tells his friends, so that they know where they can find him and award points and badges based on his perceived adventurousness.

Crowd Sourcing: This is a technique that taps into the intellectual power, opinions, contribution and collaboration of the members of a social network to develop a solution, a new idea or an opinion.

Engagement: Getting people to interact with an individual or a company in social media using a comment, a "Like" or a re-tweet.

Fan Page: This is the Facebook page a business or organization uses to connect with new people and engage with customers and other interested parties in an open dialog.

Fan: This is a person or an organization that elects to be a follower of another organization by "liking" its fan page.

Follower: This is a person or an organization that elects to be a follower of another person or organization on Twitter.

Friend: This is a self-selected entity for becoming a part of your social media community with whom you want to share your interactions, dialogs and postings.

Hashtags: Hashtags in Twitter are a community-driven convention for adding metadata to a user's tweets. They were originally developed to create groups on Twitter for tracking a topic.

Influencer: This is a person or a brand of high credibility and trust with a large social media reach (number of followers and readership).

Involvement: Getting fans and friends to interact with comments or posts or "Likes."

Like: The Like button is a tool Facebook users have to share their approval or endorsement with their network of friends. Users can Like a Page as a way of providing a recommendation or they can simply "like" an individual post, picture or video to provide a virtual thumbs up.

Reach: Number of followers or friends reached directly and via other friends.

Share: To post or re-post content on a social media site is to share it. Facebook specifically has a share option, which allows you to post someone else's content on your page. On Twitter, this is called re-tweeting.

Social Apps: Small applications (e.g., mobile, Facebook, etc.) designed to encourage interaction and social dialog to spread a product and service in a positive way with a positive sentiment.

Social Brand: Brand value in the social media.

Social Campaign: Initiatives in the social network designed to engage people in active dialog for a given purpose, generally generating a buzz and concrete interaction for a given purpose.

Social Capital: Social capital of an individual (or a company) in a social network is the ability to influence others in the network. It is a function of the size of the individual's network and the weight of the individual's voice in the network.

Social Channel: This is a virtual channel created by the network of friends and peers of your customers. They transport your messages to the customers with neutrality and with their consultative opinions that can amplify your messages. The channel also helps you to understand the genuine opinions of the customer base.

Social Commerce: Commerce that is triggered by social media dialog. This is part of electronic commerce that involves using social media that supports social interaction and user contributions, to assist in the online buying and selling of products and services.

Social Content: Content such as stories, pictures, videos, graphics, presentations, places, etc., that people care about and like to talk about and share with others. A conversation gives relevance and context to the social content and enriches it (e.g., restaurant reviews or information on a vacation destination).

Social CRM: Customer relationship management based on the dialog and analysis of conversations of people to enhance and leverage the customer relationship. Often is executed through social CRM systems.

Social Dialog: The dialog between two people in the social network consisting of two people engaged in dialog, liking or sharing things.

Social Enterprise: An enterprise in which all employees are natural users of social media in their daily lives and it operates using all the social resources of the employees in daily business.

Social Graph: Sum total of all the connections in social media. It contains friends, brands, locations, items etc. ...

Social Media Channels: These are places where people in the social network can go to interact with other users, companies, brands, content and services provided through dialog.

Social Media: Media channel providing the output of conversations, exchanges and information shared by people in social networks. This contrasts with the classical media channels like TV, newspapers, magazines and radio. The term social media is often also used to label the content generated by the social network.

Social Media Monitoring: The process of monitoring and analyzing the conversations in social media to understand what people say and to generate insights based on the conversations.

Social Network: A network of people volunteering to communicate with each other in sub-groups or in its entirety.

Social Objects: These are objects (anything: people, places, food, restaurants, books, movies, etc.) with social tagging.

Social Resource: This is the network of people you know and who share your views, which you could align to your mission and activate for your goals. This resource, which has always existed, has become far more potent because of the Internet, Web 2.0 technologies and social media platforms like Facebook, providing instant, mobile, global access and communication with a vast number of contacts.

Social Search: Searching for users, topics, products, brands and categories based on the social information that people give in their profiles and conversations.

Social Tagging: Social tags are the opinions of people attach to any object – people, places, food, restaurants, books, movies, etc. This form of tagging gives a cumulative opinion of that object.

Social: The word "social" has many meanings. In the current context, it is an adjective that means "with the participation, interaction, contribution or involvement with/from others." "Others" can be friends, peers, family or the general public.

Timeline: The chronological listing of all posts in a given feed, be it an individual's, another user's or from a list. Used by many social media platforms, such as Facebook and Twitter.

Trending: Topics on which there are many posts (hotly talked about) on Twitter in a given region.

About the Authors

Sharad Gandhi is a senior business and strategy consultant with marketing and corporate experience at Intel, IBM, Siemens and Tata. He believes that communication is one of the fundamental human motivations, born from our need to survive. He has always been fascinated by how we have leveraged technologies like computers, the Internet, mobile phones and social media to make communication richer, easier and more intuitive. Sharad holds an electronics engineering degree from the Indian Institute of Science in Bangalore and lives in Munich, Germany.

Christian Ehl is an experienced entrepreneur with a passion for technology and how it transforms our lives and the way we do business. His corporate work focuses on gaining efficiency and potential through the use of innovative technologies across the value chain and making it easy and natural for people to use those technologies. Christian is CEO of the social media consulting company Hillert und Co. Interactive and works for major corporations such as BMW, Siemens and Microsoft as well as innovative start-ups changing the business landscape. Christian holds an electronics engineering degree from the Technical University of Munich and an MBA from Wake Forrest University.

www.thesocialresource.com

authors@thesocialresource.com

CPSIA information can be obtained
at www.ICGtesting.com
Printed in the USA
LVIW011806111012

302503LV00008BA